Role of Gorkhas in Consolidation of British Rule in the North-East Frontiers

About the Auther

Dr. (Mrs.) Anjalee Muktan Shangpliang, Ph. D., Associate Professor, teaches History in Lady Keane College, Shillong and has interest in the study of origin and evolution of Khasi society, culture and education. She has done her Ph. D. on "Emergence and Role of New Social Forces in Khasi-Jaintia Society (1826-1972)", from North Eastern Hill University (NEHU) under the guidance of Prof. Manorama Sharma. Recently, she has submitted a project work on "Emergence and Role of Khasi Educated Women" under the College Teachers Minor Research Programme (MRP) of the University Grants Commission (UGC). She has edited several editions of the College magazines and History Department magazines and has published articles in the journals of the North-East Indian History Association (NEIHA) and Keanean Journals.

Role of Gorkhas in Consolidation of British Rule in the North-East Frontiers

Anjalee Muktan Shangpliang

CONCEPT PUBLISHING COMPANY PVT. LTD.
NEW DELHI-110059

ISBN-13: 978-93-5439-068-5

First Published 2022

Published and Printed by

Concept
Since 1974

Concept Publishing Company Pvt. Ltd.
A/15-16, Commercial Block, Mohan Garden
New Delhi-110059 (India)
T: 91 11 41101460, 91 11 25351460, 91 11 25351794
E : publishing@conceptpub.com, *W*: www.conceptpub.com

Cataloging in Publication Data--Courtesy: D.K. Agencies (P) Ltd. <docinfo@dkagencies.com>

Shangpliang, Anjalee Muktan, author.
Role of Gorkhas in consolidation of British rule in the North-East frontiers / Anjalee Muktan Shangpliang.
pages cm
Includes bibliographical references and index.
ISBN 9789354390685

1. Gurkha soldiers--India, Northeastern--History. 2. India. Army--Recruiting, enlistment, etc. 3. India, Northeastern--History, Military. 4. India--History--British occupation, 1765-1947. I. Title.

LCC UA842.S53 2022 | DDC 355.009541 23

Preface

This book has its genesis in my M.Phil thesis entitled—"Gorkha Recruitment in the Military and Para-military Forces in North East India (1825-1920)". On this work I further developed its scope and widened its parameters, so as to fully delineate the crucial role played by the Gorkhas and other native soldiers, in the task of unification, consolidation and formation of what is known today as the North Eastern region of India. It was with the help of superior military power that the British could expel the Burmese from the trouble-torn Brahmaputra Valley, subdued and socialised the turbulent hill tribes and united the whole North East Frontier into one single political and administrative unit called the Province of Assam.The then Chief Commissioner of Assam, Mr. Bampfylde Fuller himself admitted the fact by saying – "The task of pacifying and humanizing these primitive hill people would have been impossible had there not been at the command of the civil Government a trained and armed force which could be deployed in small detachments, could be rapidly set in movement and could make shift with a minimum of transport."[1] At the time of the British intervention, the North Eastern Frontier was a conglomeration of multiple petty kingdoms and chiefdoms with distinctive cultures, dialects and religions and the people were constantly embroiled in internecine feuds, murders and trans-frontier forays. The plains of Assam, ruled by the Ahom kings was reeling under a state of civil war and anarchy followed by Burmese incursions which only aggravated the woes and sufferings of the Assamese people. The Sadiya-Khowa Gohain and the Khamtis and more particularly the *Gauns* or the chiefs of the Singphos joined the Burmese in their plundering and slave running expeditions as far west as Jorhat. In the wake, thousands of Assamese peasants fell into their captivity.[2]

In such perilous time the British came to Assam's rescue.With the help of superior military power, the British not only defeated and expelled the Burmese from Assam but also liberated it from the extreme state of social and political turmoil. The rebellion of the Moamoriahs was quelled, the plundering of the Singphos and Khamtis were stopped and peace and order brought back to Assam. The war like hill tribes were subdued and their countries were annexed to the British territory to form a greater province of Assam. Speaking about this and referring to India as a whole, a noted historian writes—"Whatever their other faults, one thing certainly goes to the credit of Britishers that though totally alien to the soil, they managed to hold under their sway this vast subcontinent stretching from the North East, touching the Indo-Burmese border to the North West, touching the Indo-Afghan border with all its geographic, ethnic and cultural diversity having knitted into a single administrative unit."[3]

This book is, thus, an attempt at reinterpreting the history of building up of a powerful military organization in the North East through a long drawn process of recruitment, training, research and development which was made eventually capable of subjugating and taming the turbulent hill people and patching up their inter-conflicting heterogeneous countries into one consolidated province of Assam. This military organization was predominantly composed of the Gorkhas including the Hindustanis and other local recruits under various forms, ramifications and titles given to them from time to time, such as Assam Light Infantry, Sylhet Light Infantry, 42nd Bengal (Gorkha) Infantry, 44th Gorkha Rifles, Frontier Police, Military Police and the Assam Rifles.These were the powerful instruments with the help of which the British succeeded in the task of establishing their suzerainty over the hills and plains and bringing the whole of the North Eastern Frontier under one political unit. In this work I have focused mainly on the Government policy on Gorkha recruitment and their role in consolidation of British rule in the North Eastern Frontier with the view in mind that the readers, academicians and scholars who are interested on this topic may be benefited.

While writing this book I have incurred heavy obligations to a number of personalities, by way of taking their moral, intellectual and material help, and now I would take this opportunity to extend my gratitude and thanks to them.

First of all, I thank Prof. Imdad Hussain (retired), Department of History, North Eastern Hill University, who not only guided me in my M.Phil study but also helped me with many books and valuable documents without which the achievement of M.Phil degree would not have been possible.

I am grateful to many authors whose works I have extensively consulted, particularly Dr. H.K. Borpujari, Prof. A.C. Sinha, Prof. T.B. Subba, Prof. Imdad Hussain, Sir Edward Gait, Sir Alexander Mackenzie and Col. L.W. Shakespear from whose writings I have copiously drawn materials for my work. I also tender my thanks to the officer-in-charge of Shillong Record Room, the staff of Assam State Archives and many Libraries from where I have received help and co-operation.

My deepest regard and gratitude goes to my father, K.K. Muktan, (MCS Retired and author) for his constant inspiration, academic guidance and help throughout my research work. I have liberally quoted from his book, *The Legendary Gorkhas*, in this present work of mine.

My dearest mother who is no more with us today, was the one who with all her love and alacrity busied herself to cater to my needs during my M.Phil work. I deeply miss her at this moment. May her departed soul rest in eternal peace.

Shillong **Anjalee**

NOTES

1. Col. L.W. Shakespear, *History of Assam Rifles*, Forewords, pp. vii-viii.
2. Imdad Hussain, "Problem of the Frontier" published in *Comprehensive History of Assam*, Vol. IV, H.K. Borpujari (ed.) 1992.
3. Alexander Mackenzie, *The North East Frontier*, quotation at the Flap.

Contents

Abbreviations

ALI	—	Assam Light Infantry
BAAR	—	Bengal Annual Administrative Report
BJP	—	Bengal Judicial Proceedings
BPP	—	Bengal Police Proceedings
FEAP	—	Foreign External A Proceedings
FEBP	—	Foreign External B Proceedings
FPC	—	Foreign Political Consultation
FSC	—	Foreign Secret Consultation
HPA	—	Home Police A
HPB	—	Home Police B
HPP	—	Home Public Proceedings
MC(P)	—	Military Consultation (Proceedings)
RLI	—	Rangpur Light Infantry
SLI	—	Sylhet Light Infantry

Glossary

Atta	—	Wheat flour
Char-Jats	—	Four sections of the community
Gurung Kura	—	Language of the Gurungs
Havildar	—	Non-commissioned officers in the Indian Army corresponding to sergeant in the British army
Jemadar	—	Junior Commissioned officer, peculiar to Indian system
Khukris	—	The national weapon of the Gorkhas
Naik	—	Non-commissioned officer in the Indian army corresponding to corporal in the British army
Paharis	—	People from the hills
Pax batiya	—	People of western Nepal
Subedar	—	Junior Commissioned officer in Indian army
Solah-jats	—	Sixteen sections

Prologue

After the treaty of Yandaboo in February 1826 the Burmese were finally expelled from Assam, Manipur was restored back to Gambhir Singh, the Jaintia Raja, Ram Singh, was confirmed in his possessions both in the hills and the plain belts of Surma valley and Govind Chandra was reinstated as the Raja of Cachar. Thus having established political suzerainty over the vast territories of Assam, Cachar and Jaintia, the British was confronted with two major predicaments—one, the consolidation of British rule over the newly acquired territories of Assam and—two, subjugation and pacification of the marauding hill tribes of the frontier areas who were in constant war among themselves and habitually raided and kidnapped the British subjects from the plains below. To resolve these problems the Company needed to re-organize its army on a new footing and make it strong enough to adequately deal with the hill tribes and at the same time to render the military organization less burdensome to the Company's exchequer as the heavy expenditure already incurred in the war against Burmese had almost exhausted the Company's coffer. In view of this the Governor General in Council, on recommendation of the Agent, decided on March 7, 1828, to withdraw the regulars from Assam to Jamalpur. The Governor General also reduced the strength of army engaged in North East Frontier into four regiments as—(1) the First Assam Light Infantry at Gauhati (2) the Second Assam Light Infantry at Sadiya (3) the Sylhet Light Infantry in Sylhet and (4) the Bengal Infantry Battalion at Silchar.[1] For the purpose of performing ordinary duties and suppression of internal disturbances the Rongpur Light Infantry (RLI) was strengthened by addition of two companies of Gorkhas.[2] It was given the title of Assam Light Infantry with the strength of about one thousand strong all ranks.

Mention may be made here that since 1823 the Rongpur Light Infantry (RLI) was engaged in the defence of the North East Frontier and on the outbreak of the war with Burma there were three Gorkha companies fighting against the Burmese side by side with the 23rd Bengal Native Infantry, the Dinajpur Local Infantry and the Champaron Light Infantry. Thus the Gorkhas were actively involved in the whole process of military actions from vanquishing the Burmese from Ahom kingdom to the subjugating and pacifying the inhabitants of the North East Frontier. The role played by the Gorkhas in consolidation and perpetuation of British rule in the North East India have been amply reflected through the punitive expeditions carried out by them, as narrated by Col. L.W. Shakespear in his book, *History of the Assam Rifles*. Speaking about the laudable task performed by the native army in assisting the Civil authorities to subjugate and humanize the primitive hill people, Sir Bampfylde Fuller, Chief Commissioner of Assam said,—"The task of pacifying and humanizing these primitive hill people would have been impossible had there not been, at the command of the Civil Government, a trained and armed force which could be employed in small detachments, could be rapidly set in movement and could make shift with a minimum transport."[3] Commenting about the Gorkha soldiers he further writes, "It was fortunate for the Government of the province that on these emergent occasions it could rely upon a garrison of regular troops that included three Gorkha regiments."[4]

Gorkhas had shown a remarkable aptitude and capability in jungle warfare during the war with Burmese. The Chief Secretary at Fort Willams, George Swinton was very much impressed by the Gorkhas capacity to withstand the climate of Assam and their fighting skill in the mountain fastness of the North East Frontier areas. He wished that a full battalion composed of Gorkhas could be invaluable. The Gorkhas could, thus, create an impression in the minds of the British administrators that they were definitely more efficient and better soldiers in all respects than any other local recruits. Thomas Campbell Robertson, David Scott's successor and Agent to the Governor General, drew the attention of the Government of India in June 1832 to the need for restoring the Sylhet Light Infantry (SLI) to its former strength with recruitment of more Gorkhas. The Governor General, Lord William Bentinck, therefore, proposed to add to the Sylhet corps two companies of Gorkhas. Bentinck described the Gorkhas as "brave and energetic" and "the most eligible" to form the two companies. He emphasized the fact when he said, "he would gladly see them composed of Gorkhas."[5]

The Manipuris, who once dominated the roll in the ALI were no longer so highly regarded by the Commanding Officers. Their reports stated that the Manipuris "proved indifferent soldiers under the strict routine of drill and discipline to which they have a great aversion." Moreover, the reports submitted by Captain Francis Jenkins and Lieutenant Robert Pemberto cast a shadow of doubt and suspicion on the attitude of Manipuri soldiers. Their Commanders did not place much reliance on them and that the best Manipuris always preferred to serve their own Raja rather than the Company. Therefore, the number of Manipuris in the ALI gradually dwindled to mere ninety-six and that of the Gorkhas progressively increased. The battalion, during 1833-39, was composed of 1080 of all ranks organized into twelve companies of which as many as four companies or one-third of the battalion was composed of Gorkhas. The Commanding Officer, Major Adams White was keen to increase the Gorkhas and frequently sent recruiting parties to Nepal borders. Thus the number of Gorkha troops swiftly increased in all regiments and they started taking up leading roles in the punitive expeditions in the hills with remarkable success. However, it was not easy to get Gorkha recruits according to the need of the Company. The Nepal Durbar was always averse to the idea of its subjects joining the Indian army. On the issue of Gorkha recruitment Jang Bahadur, the Prime Minister of Nepal was strictly uncompromising. He took stringent measures against the Nepalese leaving the country without authority of the Durbar.

As regards the Assamese people the review report of Sir William Mansfield, Bengal's Commander-in-Chief observed that the Assamese peasants were not of the fighting classes and that they were said to be great opium eaters and totally unfit as soldiers. He, therefore, decided to replace these men, some 337 of all ranks with Gorkhas and Hindustanis who were best suited for service in Assam. About the Cacharis, the Chief Secretary in Calcutta found them to be "timid" and "effeminate" not worthwhile to be recruited. The Nagas, the Singphos, the Khamtis and other tribes were found to be "too little advanced in the art of civilization and of Government to be able to make any effectual resistance against the numerous armies of the Burmese." Thus the Gorkhas and the Hindustanis came to be recruited freely which virtually became the backbone of the regiment. Meanwhile reports had been received that the Hindustani regiments in the Khasi Hills were suffering from the effects of climate. The rigours of climate made it difficult for the Hindustanis and the Sikhs to serve in the frontiers, in fact the commanding officers found it increasingly difficult to grant furloughs to the men and at the same time to maintain too many outposts in the frontier. Hence, the Commander-in-Chief sought to reduce the number of outposts and to ensure regular and periodical relief to all regiments.[6] Accordingly Sir William Mansfield in his letter dated 1st July, 1865 recommended for the formation of one local regiment in the model of Gorkha regiment of Bengal Presidency who had always displayed greater fighting qualities than the Hindustani regiments. In order to contain the ferocious tribes in their hilly fastness Mansfield proposed to have two such regiments—one mainly of the Gorkhas and the other consisting of frontier tribes. These two corps combined with the existing regiments were considered to be strong enough to tackle the law and order situation of the frontier.

In those days there was no system of central posts being held by troops and the flanks by the Police and both were detailed indiscriminately in all posts. It was subsequently realized that the station guards and escorts did not require highly trained soldiers. To place highly trained Gorkhas as Jail or Treasury guards is a pure waste of money. Sir Elliot, the Chief Commissioner of Assam remarked, "There was no reason why for a gentle and peaceful population like the Assamese, more war like instrument (Gorkhas) should be required for such a purpose than elsewhere."[7] This policy of substituting the army by the police for lighter duties ultimately led the Government of India to constitute in March 1883, four Divisions of Frontier Police consisting of mostly the Gorkhas and they were relieved of all station duties.[8] The Frontier Police of Assam, in course of time took the title of Military Police and became the main plank in the system of defence of the North East Frontier.

Earlier after the Sepoy Mutiny in 1857 the Government formed a Royal Commission on army reform under Major General Jonathan Peel to go into the matter of Army Reform and reorganization. The

Commission submitted its report in March1859 in which it recommended—an increase in the British troops with corresponding reduction in the Indians maintaining 1 : 2 ratio between them, reorganization of Indian armies in "different nationalities and castes and as a general rule, mixed promiscuously through each regiment," and the removal of arsenals and the artilleries from Indian hands. Following this recommendation the Assam corps had been delocalized and placed in general roster of the regular infantry regiments. With this change, the 1st and 2nd ALI became respectively the 46th and 47th (Assam) Native Infantry and the SLI became the 48th Sylhet. Their strength was fixed at 600 men organized into 8 companies.

After Lord Roberts took over as Commander-in-Chief of Indian Army in 1885 who was the greatest exponent of 'Martial Class', the Gorkhas, especially Magar and Gurung were recognized as belonging to martial class. In view of difficulties in obtaining recruits from this class these were reserved for recruitment in the regular army alone and were not permitted to recruit for Assam Police. This had an adverse affect on the enrolment of the Assam Military Police and recourse had to be taken to try for more Cacharis and Jarvas, however, without much success. The problem was solved only when in 1891 a new Recruitment Depot was opened at Purnia. This Depot was later on shifted to Darjeeling itself from where good number of Gorkhas were regularly recruited. The Gorakhpur Recruiting Centre became exclusively reserved for Indian Army while the Darjeeling Depot was free for Assam's requirement.

Dealing with Hill Tribes

The Brahmaputra and the Surma valleys of Assam which constituted the plains regions of the North East Frontier, were surrounded by sub-Himalayan mountains on all sides. It was bounded on the north-west by the kingdom of Bhutan inhabited by semi-Mongoloid tribe called the Bhutias ; the territories lying on the proper northern periphery, roughly 92.40 to 95.30 degree east was the home to a number of primitive tribes like the Akas, Miris, Dufflas or Mishmis and the Abors ; on the extreme east lay the territory called Sadiya where lived a tribe called the Khamtis. Around the Patkai hills, extreme border between Assam and Burma, there lived another tribe known as Singphos. In the southern flank of the Brahmaputra river where an irregular chain of mountains runs westward from the Patkai mountain there lived the Nagas, Khasis, Jaintias and the Garos over the hills and down the southern slopes of the hills there lived another tribe called Lushais (presently called Mizos) and the Tripuris. These hill tribes had their own dialects not understandable to each other, distinct faith and culture and were "different in every conceivable way from those of India proper."[9] Numerous rivers and streams descend down from these hills and empty themselves on the Brahmaputra river in the north and on the Bay of Bengal in the south.

These tribes were always embroiled in internecine feuds among themselves. Clan warfare, group skirmishes, kidnaps and murders were the order of the day. For a minor offence or wrong committed by one community or a clan was immediately retaliated by the other clan with the same severity of punishment for the restoration of the so-called disgrace. Butler remarked, "The Singpho could not ever abandon without dishonour the application of *Lex Talionis* to one who had murdered his relative imagining that the soul of the murdered will torment him until his manes are appeased by the death of the enemies. That the anger of the deity would be roused should an opportunity of retaliation be neglected."[10] The Garos also harboured the same type of belief among them and invariably took revenge inflicting equal punishment against any harm done to them. F. Hamilton writes, "Relations of the person killed, are by custom, held bound to demand blood for blood, and ought to put to death either the murderer or one of his kindred or at least one of his slaves."[11] It is, therefore, not a rare case to see clashes and fights among the tribes of Assam always embroiled in feuds—clan against clan, family against family and individual against individual.

The Nagas were one of the most ferocious and war like tribes of Assam frontier. They would habitually raid their enemy's village at dead of night. First, they would set fire on the houses of the enemy and then attacked the fleeing inhabitants with their traditional weapons like spears and daggers. They mercilessly beheaded their enemy and carried the victims' head with a sense of great triumph and celebration. They proudly displayed the human skulls on the portals of their houses as trophies of great honour. The number of human skulls possessed by a person was considered as the symbol of his social status and honour. The Miris and the Abors also carried on nocturnal attacks, like the Nagas but the Tanae people made wars face to face with their enemies in broad day light in a show of strength.[12] The Akas cherished a stubborn attachment to their land and forest and any attempt to dispossess them was sure to be meted with strong resistance. The Akas used light spear, narrow but long swords and bows and arrows. The Khasis and Jaintias armed themselves with bows and arrows and a naked sword with shield. In the similar way, the Garos used a long but narrow sword and a shield made of thin wood.

The hill tribes of Assam did not confine their squabbling within themselves in their hilly fastness but they also came down the foot-hills and raided the markets of the plains causing frequent law and order problems for the British government. The forays perpetrated by the hill tribes caused great amount of depredation and loss of property to the peaceful British subjects living in the plains below. The Khasis were in constant state of warfare with Sylhet foothills before and after the British claimed Diwani of Sylhet. It is said that the "Khasis ravaged with fire and sword the fertile plains at the foot of their hills with impunity." A British officer wrote – "hitherto been inhabited by a race of barbarous and savage mountaineers whose aggressions have been constantly the terror of our frontiers and whose enmity and jealousy have prevented all intercourse between neighbouring districts." Night was the time that they choose for their murderous assaults when no age or sex was spared and long before the dawn of the day they returned back to their mountain fastness with plunder. The Jayantias raided on the border of Assam near Jayantiapur and carried away live-stocks and other properties belonging to the plains people. Occasionally they also kidnapped British subjects for the purpose of human sacrifice at the alter of Goddess Durga. This is stated to be the primary reason leading to the annexation of Jaintia Hills by the British in 1835. The Garos habitually raided the foothills of Mechpara and Kalumalupara of Goalpara district and carried away food-stuff and valuable belongings of the plain people. This practice of making regular raids by the hill tribes on the territories of the Assam caused a great deal of troubles and breach of peace in the locality and became a constant cause of irritation to the Government which warranted drastic action by way of punitive expeditions against the offenders. For this reason the government had to keep ready adequate military forces at different strategic stations.

British Policy Towards Hill Tribes

Initially the British government adopted a policy of non-intervention into the affairs of the tribal people of the hills. It would be wrong, said Dr. H.K. Borpujari, to conclude that British wanted to annex the hill districts of Assam but subsequently it became expedient for the British to take actions to bring the turbulent hill tribes under control in order to maintain peace and good relations with them. Dr. Verrier Elwin, a noted anthropologist, said that the policy of the British government was one of "Protection and seclusion of the hill tribes". The British intention was not to annex and rule over the hill men, but to give them a parental deal by 'pacifying' and 'civilizing' them. The Government wanted to provide them with necessary protection from the influence of the outsiders and followed a principle of applying minimum amount of interference upon their traditional way of life. The British wanted to allow them to exercise their own genius in the management of themselves according to their culture and tradition. The legal enactments made for the rest of the country could not be automatically enforced in the hill areas except when it was deemed necessary. For example, the Penal Code of India and the Criminal Procedure Code promulgated by Government of India for Indian provinces were not made applicable in the hill districts. These were to be applied in its spirit only. The trial and punishment of minor offences were left to the justice of their traditional institutions. The Government passed Bengal Eastern Frontier Regulation in 1893, especially for the sake of hill districts in order to create an Inner Line along the Assam foothills for the purpose of prohibiting any British subject living outside the hill areas from moving into or residing in the hill areas. This Regulation is still in vogue in some hill states of the North-East.

With a view to effect minimum interference in the matter of administration of the hill districts and to protect and preserve the traditional institutions the British promulgated an order called—"The Government of India (Excluded and Partially Excluded Areas) Order, 1935 and declared the districts of Naga Hills, Lushai Hills, the Sub-

Division of North Cachar and the Frontier Tracts, as Excluded areas while the districts of Garo Hills and the Khasi and Jaintia Hills (Excluding Shillong) and the Mikir Hills Tracts of Nowgong and Sibsagar district, as Partially Excluded Areas. The Excluded Areas were not to be governed by the Acts and Rules made by the Federal Legislature or the Assam Legislative Assembly but they were under the direct jurisdiction of the British governed by the Governor of Assam. The Partially Excluded Areas were under the control of the Ministerial administration, but the Governor had an overriding power when it came to exercising his jurisdiction." No Act passed by Assam or Indian Legislature could apply to the aforesaid two classes of Hill districts unless the Governor in his discretion so directs. The objective of the Government behind this policy was to protect the hill tribes from exploitation by plains people through promulgation of Acts and rules beneficial to them and to allow the hill tribes to continue their way of life according to their own tradition and culture. The British continued to follow this policy of minimum interference in the affairs of the tribal administration until India's Independence in 1947.

In pursuance of this policy of non-intervention and adaptation of the hill tribes as law abiding and peaceful subjects, the British had to adopt a long-drawn strategies of forceful subjugation and control of the primitive tribes through protracted drive of punitive expeditions and enforcement of the rule of law. This could be possible only through organization and maintenance of strong, loyal and efficient military force. In other words, the success of the British Raj in consolidating and perpetuating its rule in the North East Frontier depended entirely on the strong and well organized military force.

In this book an attempt has been made to focus on the process of recruitment and organization of military establishment in the North East Frontier by the British with special reference to the Gorkhas and to delineate the crucial role played by the Gorkhas as one of the powerful components of the military establishment, in the task of unification and consolidation of what is known today as the North Eastern Region.

The first chapter of this book gives an introduction of the ubiquitous Gorkhas and their country of Nepal. It gives a brief account of the Anglo-Nepal war, 1814-16, in which the Gorkhas lost the battle but won the hearts of the British by their bravery and fighting skill.

The British Commander-in-Chief, David Ochterlony was so impressed by the Gorkhas courage and discipline that the British went headlong with recruitment of Gorkhas right from the year 1815 even before the war ended. The chapter also highlights on the military tradition and antiquity of the Gorkhas and describes about their origin from the ancient race of Kirata who were accredited to have joined the war of Kurukshetra. It is said that Bhagadatta, the king of Pragjyotisha, (Present Kamrup district) brought one Akshouni of soldiers consisting of Kiratas (present Gorkhas) and Cinas from the Himalayas who fought against the Pandavas on behalf of Duryodhana.

The second chapter gives a brief history of the induction of the Gorkhas into the Indian Army. It deals with the process of Gorkha recruitment, initial difficulties in getting enough recruits and the agreement of mutual concession with the Nepal Durbar for regular supply of Gorkha recruits. This chapter also gives an account of the recruitment of Gorkhas in various military forces of the North East Frontier, such as Assam Light Infantry, Cachar Levy, Military Police and finally in the Assam Rifles in large numbers.

The third chapter of the book discusses exhaustively about the recruitment policies followed by the British Government in the establishment of a powerful military organization in Assam for dealing effectively with the war like and primitive hill tribes of the north-east and civilizing and pacifying them. This was a long and crucial process of recruitment, training, research and development of the sepoys belonging to various communities, like—Hindustani, Manipuri, Gorkhas, Rabhas, Cacharis, Assamese and others.

The fourth chapter brings to us the narrative description of military encounters the British had with the hill tribes by way of punitive expeditions in order to bring them under Government control. The hill tribes were always embroiled in internecine feuds and squabbles among themselves resulting in kidnapping and murder one another's men and animals. They also, habitually indulged in making trans-frontier forays into the foothills of British territory causing immense depredation of property and human life. These refractory activities of the hill people had been causing a great concern to the Government and the punitive expeditions were imperative in order to prevent and pacify them for the establishment of law and order in the country.

The fifth chapter is about the final accomplishment of the British consolidation of power in the North East Frontier of India. The East India Company and later on the British Government of India, with the help of military and diplomatic power succeeded in expelling the Burmese from Assam, annexing the whole of the hills and plains of the North East Frontier and establishing British sovereignty over them all.

The sixth chapter is the epilogue—the concluding views and comments on the whole episode about the British annexation, consolidation and unification of the entire North East Frontier into a single political and administrative unit called the province of Assam and the role played by the Gorkhas in doing this task as one of the strong and predominant force.

NOTES

1. Col. L.W. Shakespear, *History of Assam Rifles*, p. 6.
2. BSPC, 1826; July, No. 2: March 7, No. 8.
3. Col. L.W. Shakespear, *History of Assam Rifles*, pp. vii-viii.
4. *Ibid.*, p. vi.
5. FPC 23rd July, 1832, No. 9, *Minute by Governor General*, Lord William Bentinck.
6. MP, May 25, 1865, No. 137 : Adjutant General to the Secretary, Military Department, 29 April.
7. Elliot, C., *Note on the Reorganisation of Police Department in Assam*, 20 June, 1882.
8. Home Police, October 1884, No. 25-7, A. Mackenzie to the Chief Commissioner of Assam, 15 August, 1883.
9. Col. L.W. Shakespear, *op. cit.*, p. 2.
10. Butler, J., *A Sketch of Assam*, p. 84.
11. Hamilton, F., *An Account of Assam*, p. 91.
12. Dalton, F.P.P, May 9, 1845, No. 138.

MAP OF CONSOLIDATED NORTH-EAST FRONTIERS

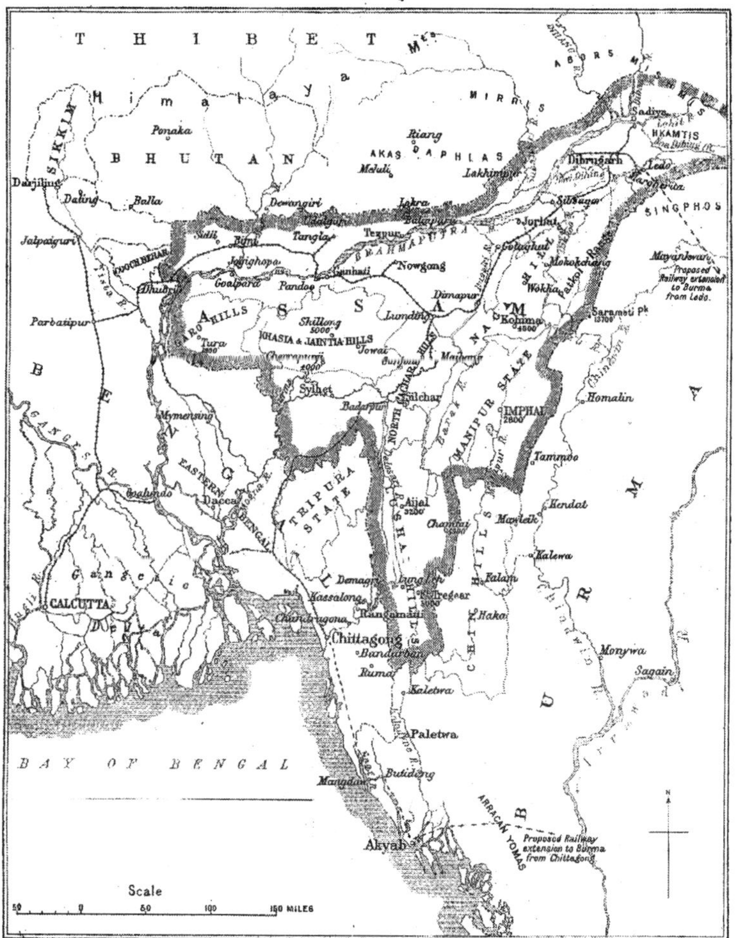

London Macmillan & Co. Ltd

MAP OF NEPAL

Showing the distribution of Martial Class recruits in Nepal

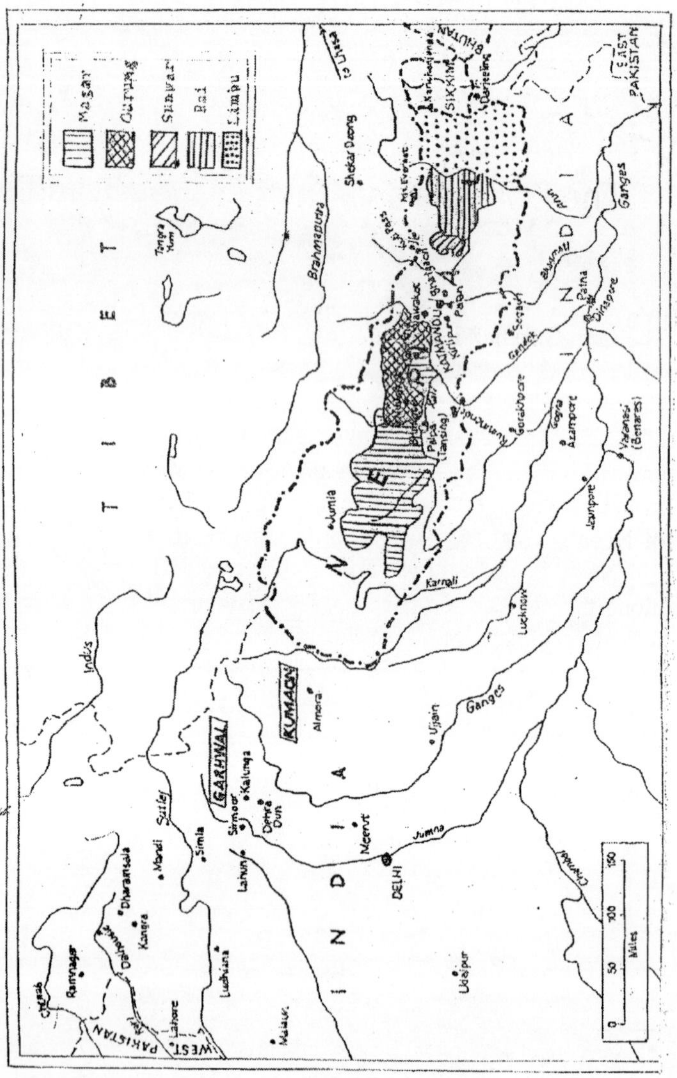

1

The Gorkhas and Their Military Tradition

The term Gorkha* is derived from two names of a small principality called Gorkha or Garakh, fifty-two miles west of Kathmandu in Central Nepal. It is today used to denote the people of entire Nepal after the Gorkha ruler Prithvi Narayan Shah (1722-75) conquered and annexed the Kathmandu valley and the neighbouring territories in the middle of eighteenth century to establish the present kingdom of Nepal.[1]

Nepal is a narrow tract of country extending for about 520 miles along the southern slopes of the Himalaya range between 80° and 88° of East Longitude. It is bounded on the north by Tibet, on the east by Sikkim and the river Mechi, on the south by East Bengal and Uttar Pradesh and on the west by Kumaon and the river Kali (Sarda). The country is often divided into three natural divisions[2]:

> The Western Divisions, or basin of the Karnal
> The Central Divisions, or basin of the Gandak
> The Eastern Divisions, or basin of the Kosi.

---

* The correct spelling is Gorkha. In February 1949 the Government of India decided to use this spelling in place of Gurkha popularized by the British. Colonel R.D. Palsokar: *History of the 5th Gorkha Rifles (Frontier Force),* (Shillong, 1991). pp. 102-103.

Nepal traditionally referred only to the Kathmandu valley and included the towns of Kathmandu, Bhatgaon and Patan. See D.R. Regmi, *Ancient Nepal* (Calcutta, 1960).

In addition to these three main geographical divisions there are two others:

1. The Nepal Valley, in which lies Kathmandu, the capital.
2. The Terai.

Nepal has offered shelter to waves of migrants for at least two millennia. Migrants have entered Nepal for security or to seek economic betterment. The earliest dwellers of Nepal are said to be of Monogoloid origin who in search of warm valleys had left their homes in the snow covered plateau of Tibet and crossed over the mighty Himalaya into the valleys of Nepal. Finding a cool and bracing climate and fertile soil they settled down and adopted the country as their own. The socially and politically dominate groups were however the descendants of high caste Hindus from India who took refuge in Nepal centuries ago. Their main sub-divisions are Brahmans and Kshatriyas—the Thakuri being the most important among the latter to which the royal house belongs and a group with numerous sub-divisions known collectively as Chettri identified by some with the Mallas who ruled the Kathmandu valley before the Gorkha conquest, but sometimes classified as Khas.[3] The most important of these sub-divisions are the Ranas, who governed Nepal as hereditary Prime Ministers for about a century till the return to power of King Tribhuvan in 1950-51. The latter part of the nineteenth century witnessed a continuous inflow of migrants from Indian plains which consisted of a large number of farmers and labourers as well as merchants and Brahmans.

Among the inhabitants of the Terai are the Tharus, a group mostly described as a mixed tribe. A far more important group however is the Newari population centred in Kathmandu valley. They are characteristically an urban group who conducted the trade and commerce of the country.[4] The remaining ethnic group of numerical importance are the Mongoloid, sometimes classed together as "Tibeto-Nepalese".[5] Among them the most prominent residents mainly in the midland area of west Nepal valley are the Magars and Gurungs—the most warlike tribes of Nepal much sought after by the British as recruits in the Indian army. Magars from the largest tribe in Nepal and constitute about one-third of the population. They are an agricultural people, cultivating their small holdings in the temperate region just north of the foothills, in the shadow of Annapurna and Machhpuchare. They were described by Lieutenant Colonel Eden Vansittart, who wrote the old *Indian Army's Handbook on Gurkhas* in 1895, as 'the basic Mongolian peasant of Central Nepal' and the *beau ideal* of what a Gorkha soldier should be.[6] Most Magars in the Indian and British armies are and have been Thapas and Puns. Puns have always been known for their broad, happy grins and British officers have even noted that none grins more broadly and is more irrespressibly cheerful than a Pun. The British welcome him as a recruit.

The Gurungs living to the north of the Magars are a more pastoral people. Like the Magars, they are divided into *Chariats* and *Solah-jats* and they are much alike in their customs and character. The Gurungs have their own language, *Gurungkura*, which is more closely related to Tibetan than any other Himalayan dialect. Colonel William Brook Northey thought the Gurungs are more intelligent and quicker in learning. They have been considersd less Hinduized than the Magars, although the Ghales, one of the four *charjats* will not touch goat or eggs and they place some restrictions on mutton. Buddhist influence is still strongly felt among the Gurungs and in time of trouble they are more likely to call in a Lama than a Brahman.[7]

Eden Vansittart, speaking of Magars and Gurungs in 1894 said:[8]

> They are intensely fond of soldiering. They are very hardy and extremely simple-minded. They are kind-hearted and generous, and as recruits, absolutely truthful. They are very proud and sensitive, and they deeply feel abused and undeserved censure. They are very obstinate, very independent, very vain and in their plain clothes inclined to be dirty. They are intensely loyal to each other and their officers in time of trouble or danger.

To the east of the valley are the Rais and Limbus, sometimes, classed together as Kiratas. According to Nepalese tradition, the Kiratas are the earliest inhabitants of the country. Driven away from central Nepal they settled in the eastern parts of the country.[9] The Rais are said to be generally smaller and quicker than the Limbus, who are slightly taller, slower speaking and have broader features. The differences in temperament between the Kiratas of eastern Nepal and the *parbatiya* of western Nepal are believed to be related to the differences in their life-styles. The *parbatiya* lives grouped together in villages in the west; they are accustomed to communal life and to meeting with friends in the evening. The Kiratas in the east live in scattered homesteads, neighbours divided by land.[10]

Among the Kiratas, nestled between Rais and Limbus is a small tribe, the Sunwar which also contributes its quota of recruits. They are generally smaller than other Gorkhas, with prominent cheek bones and raddish complexion. They are divided into many tiny subtribes but all are of a reserved demeanour and are said to have attractive manners. Unlike most other tribes, they are rarely found outside their own tribal areas.

The hills adjoining Kathmandu valley are inhabited by Tamangs, whose aboriginal tribal culture has been influenced by Buddhism rather than Hinduism. The Tamangs have been forced to support themselves as tenant farmers, day labourers and porters because of the poor quality of their land holdings. Another small tribe from eastern Nepal from which some recruits are drawn is the Tamang (also called Lama though not to be confused with Buddhist monks or priests). Unlike other Gorkhas they are more likely to be Buddhist than Hindus. They are generally industrious and amenable and occupy equal social status with the other Kirata tribe.

Tribes living in the highlands of Nepal include the Lepchas, the Tibetans or Bhote etc. Occasionally some were recruited from these groups but not often. Among the migrants the group who were more fortunate in the new environment were known as the Sherpas (literally easterner) who achieved fame for their personal qualities as well as for their capacity to endure strain at high elevation so vital to the success of Himalayan mountaineering. The counterparts of the Sherpas in western Nepal are the Thakalis who live mostly on the Tibetan trade.[11] Though the Thakalis call themselves Tamang, they have no connection with the Tamangs of Central Nepal.[12]

* * *

British contact with the Gorkhas began fairly early for the rise of the

Gorkha power and coincided with the establishment of East India Company's supremacy in Bengal. Early British interests in the region was commercial, principally in the trade that passed through the region between Bengal and Tibet.[13] In 1767 when Prithvi Narayan Shah, the Gorkha ruler who had already annexed Gurhwal and the eastern region laid siege to the three principalities in the Bagmati or Kathmandu valley and threatened the closure of this trade, the British promptly despatched an expedition to maintain the *status quo*. But the British intervention proved abortive and in 1769 Prithvi Narayan Shah overrun the valley and consolidated the three principalities along with his own Gorkha to form the kingdom of Nepal. By the time he died in 1775, his territories extended from Sikkim in the east to the Punjab hill states in the west. Gorkha expansionism, however, continued and while British interests continued to be confined to the revival of the Himalayan trade frequent border incidents took place on the southern borders. In 1814, Gorkha attack upon Butwal in the Gorakhpur district finally led to the Anglo-Gorkha war (1814-1816).

At this time the Gorkha army under Amar Singh Thapa consisted according to the Governor-General Lord Hastings estimates of 16000 fighting men and against these the Company mustered some 22000 men.[14] Hastings plan of operations was to move up four columns into Nepal, two operating from west of the river Kali and two from the east of it. The principal column from the eastern theatre under Major General Bennet Marley and consisting of 6500 men was given the task of ultimately capturing Kathmandu, while a small column under Major General John Sullivan Wood would aim at the disputed territories in the frontier and create a diversion. In the west two columns, one 4500 strong under Major General Rollo Gillespi and the other of 6500 under Major General David Ochterlony were converge upon the redoubtable Gorkha commander Amar Singh Thapa's forces.[15] Operations commenced by the advance from Meerut of General Gillespie's column over the Sewalik hills upon Dehra Dun which was captured without opposition. Further, progress was however halted by the Gorkhas at the fort of Kalanga or Nalapani situated on a hill 500 to 600 feet high and five miles from Dehra Dun. The garrison consisting of 600 men largely composed entirely of Magars (of the Purana Gorakh) under the Gorkha Commander Balbahadur, resisted two attacks of General Gillespie's forces.

Eventually, after three days of continuous shelling, the Gorkhas were compelled to withdraw and escaped through the British lines but not before killing Gillespie and killing or wounding 31 officers and 750 men in what was one of the bloodiest encounters of the war.[16]

Generals Marley and Wood fared little better than Gillespie. It was Ochterlony who had some success against the Gorkha.[17] But after Gillespie's failure in Kalanga the campaign was temporarily called off. The second campaign, of 1815, was no more a success than the first and the war dragged on. It was left to General Ochterlony in sole command of a force of 17000 men in early 1816 to retrieve the prestige of the British arms. He conducted a number of operations out-manoeuvring General Amar Singh from position to position inflicting a defeat at Jaithak and again decisively in Malaun where he was forced to capitulate on the most honourable terms. On the fall of Malaun the long and hill campaign came to an end and in March 1816 the Gorkha put their signature to the Treaty of Sagauli.

One legacy of the war that was to outlive Britain's connection with India is the Gorkha soldier. It is commonly but erroneously supposed that Britain obtained the right to recruit Gorkhas into the Indian army by the terms of the Treaty of Sagauli.[18] In reality the Company had enlisted these men long before the close of the war. From the start of the campaign the British developed a strong admiration for the fighting qualities of these short statured hillmen. One eyewitness of the assault of Kalanga thus wrote:[19]

> I never saw more steadiness or bravery exhibited in my life. Run they would not, and of death they seem to have no fear, though their comrades were falling thick around them, for we were so near that every shot told……

In early 1815 while Major General Gabriel Martindel was planning his advance from where his predecessor Gillespie left off Lieutenant Frederick Young pressed on by the Political Agent William Frasser raised an irregular force of 4500 the Sirmur hills with a view to driving a wedge in the Gorkha ranks. Though less than half of these were *Paharis*, Fraser said, "I am of the opinion that they will be found trustworthy and faithful, and always a hardworking and serviceable body." This was the genesis of the Sirmoor battalion later to become the 2nd Gurkha Rifles.[20] Even before this in late 1814 when Almora was being attacked the first elements of an irregular corps was raised from deserters by Sir Robert Colquohoun. This was the 3rd battalion.[21] At the fall of Malaun Ochterlony enrolled the entire garrison into Company's service: "I shall with the sanction and approbation of His Excellency call it the 'Nasiri (friendly) Paltan' and consider myself their commandant and patron. These trifles have very great weight; and I must confess myself sanguine in my hopes of their not discrediting my favour",[22] he wrote.

It was, however, some years before the full worth of the Gorkha battalions were realised.

Military Tradition of the Gorkhas

Soldiery is a tradition of the Gorkhas. They have adopted this martial art as their profession since the early time. The ancestors of Gorkhas, a section of whom belonged to ancient Kirata race, joined the Epic battle of Kurukshetra. The *Mahabharata* tells us that the Kiratas from northern Himalayas (Nepal) participated in the battle of Kurukshetra. It is said that Bhagadatta, the King of Pragjyotisa brought one Aksauni of soldiers consisting of Kiratas and Cinas from Himalayan country and joined the war at Kurukshetra on behalf of the king Duryodhana. They were described as brave and well accomplished in the art of fighting.

We also find mention of Kirata soldiers in the ancient literature, *Kiratarjuniyam*, who is said to have fought a war against Arjuna, the hero of *Mahabharata*. In that war Siva assuming the disguise of Kirata tribe and accompanied by a large number of Kirati soldiers fought against Arjuna and defeated him.

Another ancient literature, *Mudraraksasa*[23] speaks about the martial tradition of the Kiratas, the forebears of the Gorkhas of Nepal. It recounts that during the time of Chandragupta Maurya (c. 322-298 BC) a brigade of Kirata army was raised from north-eastern India (Nepal) through the diplomacy of Chanakya which helped Chandra Gupta to capture Pataliputra and to establish Mauryan Empire in India.

Eminent historians like Romila Thapar[24] and D.R. Regmi[25] have mentioned in their books that on the death of Harsha Vardhan in 647 AD his throne had been usurped by one Arunaswa, a Gupta prince who mis-behaved and tortured a Chinese Political Mission under the leadership of Wang Huen. In order to avenge this undiplomatic act of the Gupta prince the Chinese emperor sent an Ambassador who rushed to Nepal and raised a strong force of 700 Nepalese soldiers and 1000 Tibetan soldiers. They marched into Magadha, captured the usurper and took him to China as prisoner.

This martial tradition of the Kirati race of Nepal was further bolstered by the chivalrous Rajputs of India who came to rule over Nepal during the thirteenth century. Prithvi Narayan Shah, the scion of Rajput race, conquered the whole of Nepal and its surrounding principalities including Kirata Desh and built up a strong military nation. His government, as a matter of policy, maintained a large body of standing army whether during war or peace. Constant war and military activity were the order of the day and the spirit and morale of the army was always kept high and alert. During a few decades after his reign the Gorkhali army conquered and annexed several territories, like Kumaon, Garhwal and Sikkim in the south and Kaski, Lamjung, Noakot in the west and enjoyed absolute suzerainty over them until the treaty of Segauli in 1815.

The Gorkhas believed that fighting and dying in the battle field was the *Dharma* (pious duty) of the Kshatriyas and they willingly practiced it.[26] Most of the chieftaincies, members of Royal family and ruling class of Nepal invariably joined military service. Indulgence in arms and artilleries was considered as a royal pastime and a means of amusement by the princes.[27] Occupations other than soldiery were despised as degrading. Jung Bahadur Rana, the Prime Minister of Nepal was born of a family of soldiers. Both his grandfathers had served under General Amar Singh Thapa in Garhwal and Simla Hills from 1800 to 1816 AD. Jung Bahadur himself was posted as Jamadar at the age of fourteen, in a regiment under the command of his father. Commander Ranjor Singh Thapa, the hero of the battle of Jyathak who covered himself with glory of defeating the British army under Major Ladlow, was the son of Amar Singh Thapa, the Chief of Nepal army. Balabhadra Singh Thapa, the valiant Commander of Kalanga (Nalapani) Fort was the nephew of Amar Singh Thapa. This is, perhaps, more than enough to show how the Gorkhas, as a martial race considered soldiery as the highest and most dignified profession.

NOTES

1. Details D.R. Regmi, *Modern Nepal* (Calcutta, 1961) pp. 1-42; F. Ludwig Stiller. *The Rise of the House of Gorkha* (Patna, 1973); Bikramjit Hasrat, *History of Nepal* (Chandigarh, 1970) pp. 134-143.
2. W.B. Northey and C.J. Morris: *The Gurkhas. Their Manne Customs and Country* (London, 1928, Indian Reprint I, p. 4. For a fuller description of the land, P.P Kar and William M. Jenkins, *The Himalayan Kingdoms* (Priceton, 1963) Ch. 1 & 4; *Nepal, A Cultural and Physical Geography* (Lexington, 1960) see also C.H.K. Spate *et al. India, Pakistan and Ceylon*. The Regions (New Delhi, 1972) p. 464 ff.
3. See for example Byron Farwell. *The Gurkhas* (London, 1984) Appendix D. p. 300 ff.
4. For details on the tribes see Dor Bahadur Bista, *The People of Nepal* (Kathmandu, 1967).
5. Leo E. Rose and Margaret W. Fisher: *The Politics of Nepal* (Ithaca, New York, 1970) p. 12. According to Brain Hodgson, British Resident in Kathmandu during 1823-1843 and the earliest authority on Nepalese ethnology, the aborigines of Nepal are the Magars, Gurungs, Newars, Khambus (Rais), Yakthumba's (Limbus), Murmis (Tamangs) and Lepchas who are undoubtedly the descendants of Tibetan immigrants.
6. Byron Farwell: *op. cit.*
7. Byron Farewell *op cit*; see also Donald A. Messerschmidt. *The Gurungs of Nepal* (New Delhi, 1976).
8. Quoted in *Ibid.*
9. Ram Rahul: *The Himalayan Borderland,* (Delhi, 1970) pp. 33.
10. Byron Farewell: *op cit.* p. 300.
11. Leo Rose and M.W. Fisher: *op cit.* p. 9-13.
12. Ram Rahul: *op cit.,* p. 4.
13. Alistair Lamb: *Britain and Chinese Central Asia* (London, 1960) Ch. I; also K.C. Choudhuri, *Anglo-Nepalese Relations* (Calcutta, 1960) p. 26 ff.
14. John Pemble, *The Invasion of Nepal. John Company at War* (Oxford, 1971) pp. 126-27. By March 1815 the number of British troops swelled to 35,000 regulars and 13,000 irregulars.
15. *Ibid.*
16. Gorkhas losses were said to be 520 killed or wounded.
17. Byron Farwell, *op. cit.*, p. 29, thus comments upon the generals: "Of the four generals in charge of the columns, two were completely incompetent; they failed to reach even the outer ramparts of Nepal and were subsequently sacked. A third general Rollo Gillespie, appears

to have been not entirely same. He had received head wounds in earlier battles and it was said that his mind was unsettled by alchohol and megalomania; he was vain and impetous and harboured an intense desire for glory..."

18. There is no reference to recruitment of Gorkha in the Treaty. For its terms see Aitchison, C.U. *Collection of Treaties, Engagement, and Sunnads, Relating to India and Neighbouring Countries*. Vol. II, pp. 205-211. Calcutta. Printed by G.A. Savielle and P.M. Cranenburgh, Bengal Printing Company Limted, 1863.
19. Ensign John Shipp, quoted in Farwell, p. 30.
20. For an account of this battalion, L.W. Shakespear, *History of the 2nd King Edward's own Goorkha Rifles* (*The Simoor Rifles*). 2 vols. (Aldershot, 1912/24).
21. Nigel Woodyatt, *Regimental History of the 3rd Queen Alexendra's Own Gurkha Rifles* (London, 1929); C.N. Barclay (Ed.) *The Regimental History of the 3rd Queen Alexendra's Own Gorkha Rifles*, 2 vols. (London, 1953).
22. Quoted in Pemble, *op cit.*, p. 275. The 4th and 5th Battalions were raised during 1857-58. For development of the battalions and subsequent numbering see Appendix A.
23. *Mudraraksasa*: Translation by Satyanarayan Singh with Sanskrit and Hindi Commentaries. Ac-II. p, 89. See also the Text translated and annotated by M.R. Kali, p. 24-26.
24. Romila, Thapar: *A History of India*, Vol. I, 1966, p. 114.
25. D.R. Regmi: *Ancient Nepal*, p. 192.
26. K.K. Muktan, *The Legendary Gorkhas*, 2002, p. 23.
27. *Ibid.*

2

Induction of Gorkhas into the Indian Army

The British came in close confrontation with the Nepalese army, for the first time during the Anglo-Nepal War, 1814-16. In November 1814 the East India Company attacked Nepal from four directions at a time. The Gorkha troops, under the command of General Amar Singh Thapa fought heroically on all the four fronts and succeeded in repulsing the enemy. The British troops were twice beaten back by the redoubtable Gorkhas in the battle of Kalanga killing their army Commander, General Gillespie. Another British attack on the Fort of Jyatak on 25 December,1814 was successfully failed by Gorkhas inflicting heavy casualties to the enemy. Thirty British officers and seven hundred and eighteen men of the British perished in the counter assault of the Gorkhas. The Gorkhas fought for more than a year and a half with bravery and supreme sacrifice but could not hold on for long against the superior number of British troops. The Nepalese army could not be pitted against the overwhelming number and sophisticated weapons of the British. The war ended in favour of the East India Company—"The British won the Anglo-Nepal War but the Gorkhas conquered the hearts of the British, not of course, by their *khukuris* but by their fighting qualities, bravery and hardihood."[1]

David Ochterlony, the Commander-in-Chief of the British army was so impressed by the fighting skill and valour of the Nepalese soldiers that he remarked – "The Indian soldiers of the Company would never be able to hold their own against the Nepalese in their mountain fastness." The Gorkhas fought with so much of courage, doggedness and determination that their performance spontaneously evoked the admiration of even their enemies. Sir Charles Metcalf, a British army Commander ruefully remarked :

> "We have met with an enemy who shows decidedly greater bravery and greater steadiness than our troops possess; and it is impossible to say what may be the end of such a reverse order of things. In some instances, our troops, European and Native, have been repulsed by inferior number with sticks and stones. In others, our troops have been beaten by the enemy, sword (*khukuris*) in hand and driven miles like a flock of sheep. In a late instance of complete rout, we lost more muskets by a greater number than there were killed, wounded and missing. In short, I who has always thought our power in India precarious cannot help thinking that our downfall has already commenced. Our power rested solely on our military superiority. In this war, dreadful to say, we have had number on our side, and skill and bravery on the side of our enemy."[2]

This was the kind of experience that the British army officers had from the military encounter with Nepal which helped them to discover a hidden repository of fighting potentiality in the hill men of Nepal. The British found in the Gorkhas the right material that they had been looking for in order to bolster up the strength of the Company's army. This fact aroused a strong motivation of the East India Company to have Gorkha recruits in their army. David Ochterlony wrote to the Government expressing his desire for immediate recruitment of Gorkhas.

Besides the war like qualities of the Gorkhas there were other obvious reasons for which the British were inclined to recruit the Gorkhas in the Indian army. The British was quick to realize that the turbulent population of Nepal, well trained in warfare and itching for war and plunder, and restive for territorial expansion, as like a heap of explosives awaiting ignition. This was a danger signal for the British.[3] The shrewd British politicians were wary that even if Nepal herself remained non-aggressive and peaceful, there were many Indian native princes who could easily utilize the Nepalese military power against the British. B.H. Hodgson was confident that security of British India rested on the weakening of military strength of Nepal and that could be possible only by draining out the young population of Nepal through their recruitment in the Indian Army. Thus, induction of Gorkhas into the Indian Army would be an act of killing three birds at one stone—firstly, the warlike Gorkha recruits would enhance the strength of Indian army; secondly, draining out the *Dhakarias*[4] from Nepal through recruitment would weaken military strength of Nepal and; thirdly, the Gorkha soldiers recruited in India could be held as pledges for Nepal's good behaviour during any belligerency if so occur with Nepal.

> Thus being impressed by the Gorkhas of the Nepal army David Ochterlony, the Commander-in-Chief of the Indian Army, decided to recruit them in the Company's army. The British went a head long with the act of enlisting the Gorkha prisoners of war even before the end of the war, ostensibly, with the intention to drive a wedge into the rank and file of the Nepalese army. In early 1815 while the war was still in its peak and Major Gabriel Martindel was advancing from where General Gillespie's detachment was vanquished by the Gorkhas, Lieutenant Frederik Young hurriedly raised an irregular Gorkha force of 4500 strong from the prisoner of war camps in Dehradun, Nahan and Sirmur. It was named as Sirmur Rifles after the place name from where most of the men were drawn. This Sirmur Rifles became the 2nd Gorkha Rifles later on. At the same time with this, another battalion was raised before operation against Malaun started, to which General Ochterlony gave the name "Nasiri" meaning friendly battalion. A third Gorkha battalion was raised a few months later from amongst the Nepalese troops who were defeated at Almora. This happened due to confusion that prevailed among the Nepalese troops because, there was a talk of capitulation between the two governments towards the close of the war which lasted for more than a year.

Apart from being a good fighter, the Gorkha's other virtues, such as loyalty, honesty, hard working, tenacity and less given to social rituals etc. put them on a better stead than the Indian native soldiers working in the Indian Army. Brian Hodgson drew out a sharp contrast of the behaviours between the Gorkhas and the Indian soldiers in his report to the Government which reads:

> "These Highlanders (Gorkhas) who dispatch meals in half an hour and satisfy the ceremonial law by merely washing

> their hands and face and taking off their turbans before cooking, laugh at the pharisaical rigour of our sepoys who must bath from head to foot and make *puza* ere they begin to dress their dinner, must eat naked in the coldest weather, and cannot be in the marching trim again in less than three hours, the best part of the day. In war the former carry several days provision on their backs; the latter would deem such act intolerably degrading. The former see in foreign service nothing but the prospect of gain and glory; the latter can discover in it nothing but pollution and peril from unclean men, and terrible wizards and goblins and evil spirits."[5]

In the later years as the Gorkhas were involved in various battles and trying situations they demonstrated other virtues of great human values of honesty, tenacity and sincerity which were widely acknowledged by the British officers. In this regard Dr. Oldfield remarked:

> " ....there is not a single instance of a Nepali Chief taking bribes from, of selling himself for money to the British or any other state. This loyalty to themselves is only equalled by their loyalty to us during fiery ordeal of mutiny, the record of which, as well as of Ambeyla, of the Kabul campaign and many other wars and battles, amply testify the value of service rendered us by our Gorkha regiments incorporated in our army in 1815."[6]

This is how the Gorkhas of the little known sub-Himalayan country of Nepal began the unending story of their service in the Indian Army, nearly two centuries ago, a service of commitment, valour and sacrifice which has sanctified itself into a glorious Gorkha tradition.

Early Recruitment of Gorkhas

In the early stage, the process of Gorkha recruitment was not easy and smooth as it is today. Initially and until 1885 the Nepalese Durbar was strictly against the idea of its subjects joining the Indian Army.

The Durbar looked at every activity of the Company with suspicion and distrust and stood firm in its closed door policy to British. Right from the reign of Bhimsen Thapa down to that of Ranuddip Singh, the long period of seventy years, all the Prime Ministers of Nepal followed more or less the same policy of not allowing Gorkha recruitment in the Indian Army. In this situation, the only choice left for the East India Company was to recruit young Gorkhas clandestinely by enticing them with the help of Gorkha, Non-Commissioned Officers (N.C.Os) already in service in India. These Gorkha N.C.Os were sent to Nepal on furlough and when returning back to service they used to bring a few Gorkha young men secretly without the knowledge of the Nepal Durbar who were recruited in the Indian Army. After the fall of Bhimsen Thapa in 1837 and until Jang Bahadur Rana assumed the charge of the Prime Minister of Nepal on September 14, 1846, Nepal witnessed an anarchy and violent contest for power. During these years the British silently continued their policy of clandestine recruitment without meddling with the affairs of Nepal. Jang Bahadur always professed peace and friendship with British but he would not compromise with security of his country at any cost. He was shrewd and tactful ruler and viewed with a pinch of suspicion every overture and design of the British. He maintained strictly a closed door policy and did not allow any foreigner to enter his country. On the issue of Gorkha recruitment Jang Bahadur was strictly non-committal. He never agreed with British nor frankly be excused for fear of displeasure of the British and always kept himself aloof. Inside his country he took stringent measure against the Nepalese leaving the country without authority of the Durbar.

The process of clandestine recruitment involved great fear of suffering legal punishment on the part of the Gorkha N.C.Os, as well as running the risk of straining political relations with Nepal for the Government of India. Despite a few cases of detection and punishment by the Government of Nepal, the process of recruitment by clandestine method continued till 1858 by which time the total number of Gorkha battalions in Indian army rose to five. In 1885 the Government of India succeeded in getting the consent of the Nepal Durbar to officially recruit Gorkhas on a stipulated number through an Agreement of Mutual Concession. According to this Agreement of Mutual Concession, Ranuddip Singh, Prime Minister of Nepal agreed to supply 5600 Gorkha recruits to India annually in exchange of which Lord Dufferin, Viceroy of India agreed to give to Nepal one rifle against each recruit and also allow facilities to import chemicals for ammunition. Immediately after the agreement a recruitment depot was formally set up at Gorakhpur, Indo-Nepal border town, through which regular recruitment of Gorkha boys started. With the easy availability of Gorkha recruits the British became more selective in the quality of recruits. In 1885 Lord Frederick Robert took over as Commander-in-Chief of Indian Army who was great exponent of 'Martial Class' theory and consequently the Gorkha sepoys came to be categorized into martial and non-martial class—whereby Limbu, Rai, Magar and Gurung were considered as martial class. These four categories of recruits were exclusively reserved for enlistment in the Indian Army and the rest of the Gorkha recruits were allowed to be taken in other para-military organizations. In order to tap the Gorkhas of martial class the British opened another Recruitment Centre at Darjeeling from where Rai and Limbu recruits could be easily available. The Kiratis of the eastern Nepal, the Magars of the western Palpa district and the Gurungs of central Nepal were the much haunted lots among the Gorkha recruits for the Indian Army. The process of Gorkha recruitment increased speedily. By the year 1908 the Gorkha Brigades reached the highest peace time strength of twenty battalions.

The wake of the First World War necessitated large scale recruitment of troops, the choice for which fell squarely on the Gorkhas. In 1914 there were already some 26,000 Gorkhas serving in the ten regular Gorkha regiments that formed the Gorkha Brigade of the Indian Army. To re-inforce this existing Gorkha Brigade more than twice the number were recruited during the period of the First World War. In all, the total number of Gorkhas who left Nepal to serve the foreign emperor in one way or another between 1914 and 1918 exceeded 200000.[7] Chandra Shamsher Rana, Nepal's Prime Minister, came out of his way to help India in her war effort. The massive Gorkha recruitment that was done almost drained out Nepal of its best male population. It is said that the agricultural operation of the little sub-Himalayan country almost came to halt during the war time.

The Second World War witnessed yet another surge in the Gorkha recruitment. Juddha Shamsher, the Prime Minister of Nepal, responded magnificently to the call of the British in war preparation. The Gorkha regiments expanded all time high pushing the total strength from twenty battalions to forty-five, more than double the original strength.

After India attained Independence in 1947 there arose the question as to how the Gorkha Brigade is to be recruited. The British expressed a keen desire to retain the Gorkhas in their army who served them so well over a century. The Government of Great Britain came up with a formal proposal of retaining a few Gorkha regiments in the British army to be used in the strategic areas of South East Asia for protecting the interest of the Commonwealth. Field Marshall, Montgomery visited India personally with the mission and met Jawaharlal Nehru, the Prime Minister. He also met the King of Nepal and his Prime Minister as it was necessary to obtain the approval of the Government of Nepal for overseas services of the Gorkhas. Moreover, the permission for future recruitment of Gorkhas to maintain the required strength of the regiments was to come from Nepal itself. The Government of Nepal, true to her time honoured bond of friendship with Britain and India had no hesitation in accepting the proposal, provided Government of India had no objection to spare the Gorkhas. So, Nepal gave India all the options to settle up the matter with Great Britain. She, however, laid down conditions that the Gorkhas to be taken for overseas services should not be forced to go against their will and that they should not be used against the Hindus or to suppress unarmed men in times of civil commotion or unrest. Thus having agreed upon the conditions imposed by Government of Nepal, the Brigade of Gorkhas was broken up into two halves and shared between the Government of India and Great Britain. Out of the existing ten Gorkha regiments the 2nd, 6th, and 10th Gorkha Rifles together with two battalions and a regimental centre each were allotted to Britain to form part of the British Army, while the remaining six regiments viz., the 1st, 3rd, 4th, 5th, 8th and 9th Gorkha Rifles together with two battalions each and a Regiment Centre were retained by the Government of India. Accordingly, a Tripartite Agreement was signed in July 1947 between India, Nepal and Great Britain.

Today, the recruitment of Gorkhas in the Indian Army as well as the British Army is governed by the tripartite agreement signed among Nepal, India and Great Britain in July 1947. The agreement expressly provides that the Gorkha soldiers shall not be used against Hindu organization, unarmed mobs in civil commotion and against, of course, Nepal.[8] According to the second clause of the agreement Great Britain shall continue to recruit Gorkhas for the British army only after the requirement of such recruits for Indian army has been satisfied. Thus, recruitment of Gorkhas for Indian army has been given first preference against the recruitment for British army and this provision stands out as a symbol of age-old bond of peace and friendship between India and Nepal.[9]

Nepal has followed this tripartite agreement in letter and spirit ever since then despite pressure applied on her by China and Pakistan to terminate or modify it on several occasions. During Indo-Pakistan war in 1965 the Government of Pakistan put pressure on Nepal to stop allowing India to use Gorkhas against her, contending that Nepal being a close neighbour to Pakistan it would be morally unfair on her part to help India with military manpower against Pakistan. In 1962 Chinese aggression of India it was the formidable Gorkhas who pinched the Chinese most in Kashmere front. China lodged a complaint to Nepal for committing breach of Nepal-China agreement of friendship by allowing India to use Gorkhas. The Chinese Government has been exercising constant pressure on Nepal to extend to her similar facilities of Gorkha recruitment showing the ground that she had a political relations with Nepal much older than the British had and that she is geographically closer to Nepal than the British. But Nepal has remained firm on the Tripartite agreement.

Introduction of Gorkhas into the North East Frontiers

The introduction of the Gorkhas into the Company's affairs in the North East is marked by the Anglo-Burmese war of 1824-26. At the outbreak of the war there was already a corps named Rongpur (Local) Light Infantry serving in the North East which was composed of Gorkhas, Hindustanis and others. The services of this Infantry was placed in Assam in the wake of mounting tension with the Burmese in August 1822.[10] In 1824 the Sylhet Light Infantry (SLI) was quickly raised out of Manipuris at the request of David Scott when military occupation of Cachar became an urgent necessity in order to expel the Burmese from Assam.[11] Apart from these forces there were a bulk of other Company's forces which were composed of locals like Assamese, Cacharis, Jarvas etc. The three important military organizations which were closely associated with the affairs of the North East ever since the initial period of its political transition, consolidation and formation into British province, were—the 1st Assam Light Infantry, the 2nd Assam Light Infantry and the Sylhet Light Infantry. It will be pertinent here to give a brief account of their origin, development and transition into the present form and title of these forces for the benefit of the readers, as it often leads to confusion.

The 1st Assam Light Infantry began its life as "Cuttack Legion" raised in the year 1817 at Choubiaganj for the protection of the Cuttack district and in 1823 it was moved to Rongpur where it was renamed as Rungpur (Local) Light Infantry. It was then posted in Assam during the war with Burmese in 1822. Four years later, after expulsion of Burmese from Assam it became known as "First Assam Light Infantry" and was posted in Assam. In 1864 its title was further changed to that of "42nd Bengal Infantry (Gurkhas)" according to the numbering of the regiments of the Indian army, which ultimately became the 6th Gurkha Rifles in 1903.[12]

The 2nd Assam Light Infantry originated from the Sebundy Corps which was raised in 1835 as an irregular corps in Gauhati and was stationed in Sadiya in order to deal with Khamti and Singpho uprising. After eight years this corps changed its title to the 2nd Assam Light Infantry on being brought on to the strength of the Bengal Army. In 1864 it became known as the 43rd Bengal Infantry (Assam) and after two other slight changes it received the present title of 2/8 Gurkha Rifles.[13]

The Sylhet Light Infantry was raised in 1824 as already mentioned above. After the Burmese war, it was renamed as 44th Sylhet Light Infantry in 1864 on being incorporated into the Bengal Army, then in 1901 this regiment became known as the 44th Gurkha Rifles and again in 1907 the name was finally changed to the 1/8 Gurkha Rifles. All these regiments were mixed composition with Gorkhas from their inception and gradually the Gorkhas replaced other communities, until in the last stage when they became the 6th and 8th Gurkha Rifles they were purely composed by the Gorkhas. These regiments served entirely in Assam and Burma until 1899, taking part in every border expedition, after which they were sent to serve in other parts of India.[14]

At the time of the Sepoy Mutiny in 1857 the strength and distribution of local crops in Assam were as follows:[15]

Sylhet Light Infantry	—	800 men stationed at Cherrapunjee
1st Assam Light Infantry	—	1000 men Dibrugarh
2nd Assam Light Infantry	—	1000 men Gauhati

The Police Militia consisted of the following:[16]

Lakhimpur Police Militia	—	160 men at Dibrugarh
Nowgong Police Militia	—	150 men at Asalu
Sibsagar Police Militia	—	100 men at Jorhat.

The Gorkhas found preferred employment in both the above army corps and the police militias. Captain Charles Holroyd was particularly an admirer of the Gorkhas and to attract them he raised the pay of Police Militia men from Rs. 4 to Rs. 5 and 4 annas per month.[17] The Gorkhas, thus, predominated in all the forces. From about the middle of 1830 there began a gradual shift in the recruitment policy of the local corps the Gorkhas replacing the Manipuris, Hindustanis and other local communities. Captain John Bryan Neufville, the Commanding Officer and Political Agent for Upper Assam had always preferred Gorkha. He said:

> "Proverbially brave, active and capable of enduring fatigue both in the hills and jungles and free from the prejudices which the Hindus of regular troops were invariably accustomed.[18]

In 1835 a new militia named Cachar Levy, was raised by Mr. Grange with an initial strength of 750 of all ranks which was intended to be placed on a better footing than the ordinary police for performing military duties in maintenance of internal peace and security. With the passage of time, this semi-military force rose from strength to strength, and changed its name from Cachar Levy to Frontier Police in 1862. From 1875 onwards the Frontier Police came to be re-organised into a systematic force and gradually increased in strength. Till 1875 the total strength of Assam Frontier Police was 24000 of all ranks and it was raised to 33000 by the end of 1882. Earlier in 1879 a separate force of Frontier Police of 3000 strong was raised with Gorkha recruits and posted at Tura, Garo Hills. In 1882 the Frontier Police was renamed as Assam Military Police and arranged in a number of battalions to be placed in each territory like Naga Hills battalion, Lakhimpur Battalion, Surma Valley Battalion and Garo Hills Battalion. The organization having gradually assumed the character of a well-knit military force, in 1885 its uniforms were changed from green to khaki, distinctive silver buttons and cap badges with each battalions' name and crossed khukri badges were introduced[19]. The badge of two crossed *khukris* replacing that of inverted bugle was introduced for the first time to indicate the predominance of the Gorkhas. The Subedars wore two crossed khukris on each shoulder strap while the Jemadars rank wore only one *khukri*. Eventually, this organization came to be known as Assam Rifles in 1917. By the beginning of the First World War the organization was expanded to four battalions and its class composition was three-fourths of Gorkhas and one-fourth of Jarvas and other tribes. In order to facilitate recruitment, a recruiting depot was established at Sylhet in 1865 which enlisted large number of Jarvas and Gorkhas. This depot continued to function for some twelve years after which it was closed down.

The Gorkhas in both Assam Frontier Police as well as in the regular army showed their mettle in every war front and punitive expeditions against the hill tribes by dint of their hardihood, tenacity and bravery. They proved especially suitable for jungle warfare in the north east. The difficult terrain of Assam, "the tangled mass of vegetation, closely matted thickets of bamboo, thorny canes and creepers or the river torrents and mountain gorges" — nothing was impenetrable for the redoubtable Gorkhas.

As Assam Military Police expanded gradually and the preference fell mainly on the Gorkhas, a large number of them came to be enlisted every year by eliminating and stopping recruitment of certain communities or classes of Sepoys. "Eventually the composition of each battalion came to be three-fourths the strength of Gorkhas, and one-fourth of Jarvas, or as near that as possible."[20] However, this ratio of class composition could not be maintained for long because of the prohibition imposed by the Government of India in 1887 in recruiting the martial classes of the Gorkhas (Rai, Limbu, Magar and

Gurung), who were reserved for recruitment in regular Indian Army. This had an adverse affect on the enrollment of Assam Military Police. Ultimately, the situation was resolved to some extent in 1891 when a new Recruiting Depot was opened at Purnia near the foot of Darjeeling for recruitment of Gorkhas. In 1910 a further increase in the strength of Military Police was effected as a result of withdrawal of regular army who were looking after border areas of Assam. This led the total strength of the force to eight companies with the following class composition:

Gorkhas pure	— (4 companies)	All eight companies
Jarvas/Gorkha	— (3 companies)	comprised of 50 %
Cacharis/Gorkha	— (1 company)	Gorkhas.

In 1913 further expansion was effected in the Assam Military Police with the creation of a new battalion named as Darrang Military Police. In 1915 another Recruiting Depot was established at Gauhati with a Recruiting Officer located at Shillong Headquarters with a view to enlisting local Gorkhas settled in Assam. This measure had to be taken because of the fact that the Government of India had once again objected to recruitment of additional companies of Gorkhas. Assam met the objection by an assurance that they no longer wished to recruit from Nepal, as there was a large number of Gorkha residents in Assam from whom recruits would be obtained. In this connection the Government of India agreed to the proposal of Assam to recruit which opined — "There is no objection from the point of view of Government of India to the recruitment of Gorkhas who are genuine residents of Assam."[21]

During the First World War, 1914-18 the Assam Military Police took active part in various war fronts fighting side by side with the Gorkha Rifles of the Indian army to which it was attached. From 1915-16 the Assam Military Police started sending drafts to the regular army. By early February 1917, 2788 officers and men were supplied and by January 1918 altogether 3162 drafts had been despatched.[22] They fought gallantly against France, Egypt, Mesopotamia, Gallipoli, East Africa and earned a name for themselves. As a mark of recognition of the excellent service rendered by the men of Assam Military Police the Government of India sanctioned the old title to be changed to Assam Rifles in October 1917. The Government of India wrote to the Chief Secretary of Assam:

> "To give more prestige to the force and to raise the status and *spirit de corps* of the officers and men, these battalions might be designated as "Assam Rifles" in place of Military Police without altering their status as a civil force."[23]

As a result the Lushai Hills battalion became the First Assam Rifles, the Lakhimpur battalion the 2nd, the Naga Hills battalion the 3rd and the Manipur battalion as the 4th Assam Rifles. Ever since then the Assam Rifles witnessed steady expansion in its formation and enrolment with proportionately greater number of Gorkhas. In 1922 it had five battalions with total strength of 4093 men of which 3194 were Gorkhas. The following Table shows battalion-wise class composition of the five battalions of Assam Rifles with the enrolment of each class. From the figures mentioned in the Table it is seen that the numbers of Gorkha recruits are the highest in all the battalions leading to the total percentage of Gorkhas to 78.03.

Table: Percentage of Gorkha recruits in battalions[24]

Battalions	*Gorkhas*	*Jarvas*	*Hill Tribes*	*Others*	*Total*	*P.C. of Gorkhas*
1st Battalion	762	48	39	3	852	89.44
2nd Battalion	647	137	1	9	794	81.48
3rd Battalion	592	166	35	38	831	71.24
4th Battalion	614	108	79	2	823	79.60
5th Battalion	552	200	38	3	793	69.60
Total	**3194**	**659**	**192**	**55**	**4093**	**78.03**

Thus, the Assam Military Police which traces its origin in the Cachar Levy of 1835, having been christened as the Assam Rifles in 1917 grew from strength to strength to be a gigantic para-military force with forty-six battalions as on 2013 and still holds the same name with all pride and glory. When Assam Rifles Manual was framed by the Government of Assam the ideal class composition of the Assam Rifles was fixed as follows:[25]

1st (Lushai Hills) Battalion

Gorkhas	-	50 %
Jarvas/Cacharis etc.	-	37.5 %
Lushais	-	12%

2nd Lakhimpur Battalion

Gorkhas	-	62.5 %
Jarvas/Cacharis/others	-	37.5 %

3rd (Naga Hills) Battallion

Gorkhas	-	50 %
Jarvas/Cacharis etc.	-	37.5 %
Nagas	-	12.5 %

4th Battalion

Gorkhas	-	50 %
Jarvas/ Ahoms etc.	-	37.5 %
Kukis	-	12.5 %

5th Battalion

Gorkhas	-	50 %
Jarvas/Cacharis etc.	-	50 %

The above principle incorporated in the Assam Police Manual was closely followed by the Government of Assam down the line until the British left India in 1947.

After Independence the Assam Rifles was made more independent with its own Director General. The Gorkhas had also the distinction of having had their own officer Col. Siddhiman Rai as the Inspector General of Assam Rifles, the head of the organization. He was also the first Indian officer to hold the highest post of the Assam Rifles after the retirement of European Inspector General, Mr. Bartly in 1948. It may be noted here that before independence Assam Rifles was placed under the leadership of Civil Police with Inspector General of Police as its head.

The strength of Assam Rifles was also increased by raising more battalions and the rank of the force Commander was also upgraded to that of Lieutenant General deputed from the regular Indian army. The 6th Battalion of the Assam Rifles was raised at Tripura in 1950 and with its expansion the number of Gorkhas reached the height of 64 per cent in the organization as a whole. The community-wise percentage at that time was—Gorkhas 64, Assamese tribals 34, and others 2.

Today Assam Rifles stands as a huge para-military force with 46 battalions and performs multifaceted duties including internal peace and security, counter insurgency and border security operations. In times of war it can also be used as force under the control of the army. During peace time the Assam Rifles helps the civil authorities in rescuing people from flood havoc, earthquakes and other natural calamities. It also protects life and property of the people during political agitations and insurgencies. Thus they have become the real friends of the people. In the words of Verrier Elwin the Assam Rifles jawans are—"The custodians of law and order, pioneers of every advance into interior, the guardians on borders and above all the friends of the hill people."

NOTES

1. K.K. Muktan, *The Legendary Gorkhas*, 2002, p. 1.
2. Thompson and Garratt, *Rise and Fulfilment of British Rule in India*, pp. 256-75.
3. K.K. Muktan, *op. cit.*, p. 46.
4. *Dhakarias* are the trained soldiers of Nepal who are temporarily off the roll of Nepal army and ready to be re-employed when occasion arises. According to Hodgson there were no less than 30,000 Dhakarias in Nepal belonging to Khas, Magar and Gurung tribes (the chief military tribes of Nepal). If these Dhakarias could be obtained that would be most highly prized soldiers for Indian Army.
5. B. Hodgson: *Report to the Government, Selections from Records of the Government of Bengal*, No. xxxvii.
6. Francis Tucker, *The Story of Gorkhas of Nepal*, 1957, p. 94.
7. David Bolt, *Gurkhas*, 1967, p. 90.
8. K.K. Muktan, *op. cit.*, p. 66.
9. *Ibid.*, p. 68.
10. Imdad Hussain, "Soldiers and Settlers: Recruitment of Gorkhas", in *The Nepalis in North East India*, 2003, Ed. A.C. Sinha and T.B. Subba, p. 68.
11. Imdad Hussain, "Shan Militia: Origin of the Para-military System in Assam", in *Studies in the History of North East India*, (Ed.) J.B. Bhattacharjee, 1986, p. 145.
12. L.W. Shakespear, *History of Assam Rifles*, 1929, p. 6.

13. *Ibid.*, p. 7
14. *Ibid.*
15. Imdad Hussain, "Soldiers and Settlers: The Recruitment of Gorkhas", in *The Nepalis in North East India*, (edt.) A.C. Sinha and T.B. Subba, 2003, p. 77.
16. *Ibid.*
17. BJP, 12 April, 1855, No. 160, Robert Campbell to Jenkins, 17 February.
18. FSC 10 November, 1826: Nos. 1-22, Neufville had actually recommended a special frontier force composed of Gorkhas, Manipuris and Shans.
19. Colonel L.W. Shakespeare, *History of the Assam Rifles*, 1929, p. 56.
20. *Ibid.*, p. 57.
21. No. 152, G.W. Gwynne to Chief Secretary, Assam, 21 March, 1921.
22. H. Police A.P. November 1918, Nos. 95-96, J.E. Webster, Secretary, Government of India, Home Department, 12 August, 1918.
23. HP AP April 1920, Nos. 220-231: GOC 8th (Lucknow) Division to the Chief Secretary of Assam.
24. Imdad Hussain, "Soldiers and Settlers: The Recruitment of Gorkhas," in *The Nepalis in North East India*, (edt. A.C. Sinha and T.B. Subba) 2003, p. 87.
25. *Assam Rifles Manual*, Chapter VII, p. 51.

3

British Recruitment Policies in the North-East

Recruitment under the Company

During the winter of 1824-25, at the height of the Anglo-Burmese war (1824-26), the future defence of Bengal's Eastern frontier became a subject of detailed discussions in Fort Williams in Bengal. The hopes[1] entertained by the Governor General in Council that the states in the Eastern Frontier when restored to their native Princes would form a barrier to future Burmese expansionism had receded with reports coming in of the military incapability of their inhabitants. David Scott, Agent to the Governor General, North East Frontier since November 1823, and the originator of this policy and who had conveyed to the authorities in Fort Williams these sentiments in a series of reports to the Chief Secretary in Calcutta in November 1824.[2]

> The Assamese and Cacharis are unfortunately so timid and effeminate a character that the defence of those countries however necessary for the security of our own territories must be provided for in great measure by extraneous means.... the Nagas, the Singphos, the Khamtis and other tribes to the eastward of Assam are perhaps too little advanced in the art of civilisation and of government to be able to make any effectual resistance against the numerous armies of the Burmese.

Bengal's Commander-in-Chief, Lieutenant General Sir Edward Paget took up the question of military defence of the Eastern Frontier in the following month. Since, the early years of the century local corps in addition to regular infantry battalion had been raised for duties in difficult and particularly in unhealthy situation.[3] At the outbreak of the Anglo-Burmese war there were several such local battalions, including the three Gorkha corps. In 1824 the Rangpur local battalion subsequently made into Light Infantry was raised from the Cuttack Legion and the Sylhet Provincial battalion.[4] In February 1824 on the recommendation of David Scott, the 16th or Sylhet Local Corps was raised from immigrant Manpuris for the defence of Cachar.[5] General Paget had found the local battalions extremely useful in the Presidency as relieving the regular Bengal Native Infantry Battalions (BNI). But he had strong misgivings about the Sylhet Light Infantry (SLI) and the Arakan local battalion raised at the same time as the Sylhet corps from the Maghs of Chittagong. He argued that these regiments were composed of men who were driven out of their countries by the Burmese against whom they would be required to defend the Frontier.[6] He, therefore, submitted to the Government of India a proposal to entrust the defence of the Eastern Frontier to overseas troops.[7] His colleagues in the Council including Lord Armherst, however, were inclined towards the local corps and even in the recruitment of the frontier tribes. Out of these discussions a proposal came to be made about expanding the Gorkha battalions for service in Eastern India.[8] Sir Edward Paget was not certain if such troops would be useful in the unhealthy frontier. The Adjutant General thus wrote to the Government of India:[9]

> It appears to the Commander-in-Chief very improbable that men accustomed to the pure air and temperate climate of the hill countries in which these people are accustomed to serve, would be able to preserve their health and continue efficient for any length of time in low and marshy situation.

The subject of the Gorkha battalion was not pursued any further even though the Resident at Kathmandu confidentially reported that ready material would be available for the Company's Forces. But the Government of India decided to entrust to the local corps, the Sylhet and the Rangpur Light Infantry (RLI) for the defence of the eastern frontier.[10]

Early Policy

It was, however, not before 1828 when arrangements for the military defence of the eastern frontier was completed. In 1828 lower Assam was annexed and while the restoration of an Ahom Prince in upper Assam was kept in obeyance the frontier areas to its east was brought under effective British control.

To perform the ordinary military duties of the province and the suppression of internal disturbances the Government of India decided to strengthen the RLI by the addition of two companies. Captain Neufville sought to raise the two companies of Gorkhas through drafts from the existing Gorkha Companies of such men as could be entertained without prejudice to their standing in the line, and completed by drafts from other corps or levies. This arrangement would prevent delay and would have a good effect by retaining the promotions and opportunities in the regiment.[11] With this addition the RLI was localised in Assam and took the designation of Assam Light Infantry (ALI). Its sanctioned strength was one thousand and had, besides, an attachment of artillery. Its Headquarters was fixed at the Biswanath Cantonment, two hundred miles east of Gauhati. To guard the frontier areas about Sadiya, two companies were posted therein with a couple of gunboats each carrying a twelve pound cannon made managed by Indian *Golanauz*.

The ALI was largely composed of men from the Upper Provinces who had been restive since some time past about their prolonged employment in North Eastern Frontier. The news of their localisation in the remote region came as a surprise. When the Government of India further decided to withdraw certain allowances which they had been enjoying in Assam since the Anglo-Burmese war there was great dissatisfaction in the ranks. The Government of India at once realised the need to recruit more local men into the battalion. At any rate, the climate of the frontier had proved to be inhospitable to the constitution of the old north Indian recruits. In August 1828, Captain Neufville, therefore, informed the Government of India his willingness to recruit the entire battalion from Manipuris. The few he had entertained had proved excellent soldiers and these with the Gorkhas and Jarvas of lower Assam whom David Scott had recommended could make the battalion entirely independent of the need to recruit from outside the region. The Government of India at once agreed to Neufville's suggestion and sanctioned as '*batta*', one rupee to each private and a corresponding increase in the native officer grades to attract Manipuris. In November, two complete companies of Manipuris from the SLI were transferred to the Assam Corps as a nucleus to the further enlistment of their countrymen.

Gorkhas: Gradual Shift

The Sylhet corps remained at its peace time establishment of eight companies of eighty men each the bulk of whom were Manipuris. From the middle of 1830 however reactions set in against these men. The Manipuris in Cachar were strongly suspected to be directly or indirectly involved in the murder of the Raja Govinda Chandra.[12] Some of the local officers even expressed doubts if the Manipuris in the SLI would remain loyal to the British in the event of a clash with Raja Gambhir Singh, the Manipuri Chief who was known to be sympathetic towards his countrymen in Cachar. Even the Commanding Officer Captain Frederick Lister who had virtually ruled out the defection of his men considered it prudent to reduce the Manipuri element to 200 by replacing 150 of them by Gorkhas. The Agent to the Governor General supported the Commanding Officer and after a thorough examination of the question the Government of India allowed a gradual introduction of Gorkhas in place of the Manipuris.[13]

Meanwhile the duties of the corps remained exceedingly heavy. Ever since the uprising of the Khasis under Tirot Singh in 1829[14] a large portion of the battalion was required for operations in those hills. From 1830 detachments had to be sent to Cachar which, following its annexation in 1832, had to be considerably increased for its military occupation. Thomas Campbell Robertson, David Scott's successor, an Agent to the Governor General, North East Frontier, drew the attention of the Government of India in June 1832 to the need for restoring the SLI to its former strength.[15] In Fort William discussion at once began not only on the question of increase to the battalion but also on the material to be recruited.

The Chief Secretary at Fort William, George Swinton drew the attention of the Government of India to the possibility of raising one or two companies of irregulars to be associated with the SLI. Such irregulars had shown a remarkable aptitude for jungle and hill warfare in the Khasi Hills operations. A battalion composed of these and the Gorkhas could in the opinion of Swinton, be invaluable in Bengal and even overseas.[16] Lord William Bentinck who went over these proposals in great detail recorded a minute in July 1832 declaring:[17]

> I confess, however, I am partial to what are called local corps, a partiality I account for, partly from the favourable specimen which the hill or Gorkhas Corps are partly from their being a cheap description of force, and partly from their serving, in their department, as a counterpoise to the regular sepoys, whilst too they seem to garrison well the districts where they are placed, they are available for service in neighbouring province.

Bentinck, therefore, proposed to add to the Sylhet Corps, two companies of Gorkhas. These he described as "brave and energetic" and "the most eligible….to form the two new companies and I would gladly see them composed exclusively of Gorkhas."[18] Regarding the manner in which they were to be recruited hints could be taken, the Governor General said, from the system followed by Captain Neufville in forming the Gorkha Companies of the ALI. The commissioned and non-commissioned ranks could be had from the Nassiri and Sirmoor (Gorkha) battalions. It was also likely that these officers would bring in their comrades from their own battalions or men from the disbanded Kumaon battalion.[19]

Even as measures were taken to implement the Governor-General's minute further reports about the unsuitability of Manipuris came in. During August-October Captain Francis Jenkins and Lieutenant Robert Pemberton submitted their elaborate reports on the North East Frontier which clearly showed that the Manipuris as a soldier were no longer so highly regarded. Their inquiries had shown that subsequent Commanding Officers did not place much reliance on them and that, the best Manipuris always preferred the services of their own Raja. Their conclusion was:[20]

> although individuals of superior military qualities might be picked out from amongst the Munipoories…. generally

> speaking they would prove indifferent soldiers under our strict routine of drill and discipline to which they have a great aversion; for the description of guerrilla warfare they are constantly exposed in their own country they are ordinarily adopted and inferior to no other troop....the finest classes of men infinitely prefer the military service of their own prince with its comparatively lax discipline to our and the knowledge that they were distrusted by their immediate superior has tended to deteriorate the standard not only of the classes who would have entered into our services but to wound the spirit of those who are already in it.

Irregulars

From the middle of the 1830s widening contacts with the Hill tribes and the need to maintain outposts on the frontier led to a further development of the local forces. The Burmese problem, fear of an actual invasion or Burmese inspired tribal unrest, continued to haunt the authorities for years after the Treaty of Yandabo (1826). The Sylhet and Assam Light Infantry battalions taking the place of the regular Bengal Regiments had to be kept in the highest state of preparedness. It was extremely difficult for the local corps to maintain efficiency to take the field at a moment's notice and undertake at the same time the defence of an extensive frontier against tribal depredations. Most of the outposts were located in extremely unhealthy areas, in situations injurious to the health and discipline of the men. For years, therefore, reliance had to be placed on the irregulars for frontier duties. Their origin dates back to the days the Ango-Burmese war. A small Sebundy corps, drawn from Jarvas of Lower Assam with a few Gorkhas and Hindustanis, existed for duties of the Garo frontier since the 1790s.

In the ALI the Manipuris gradually dwindled to a mere ninety six and the Gorkhas progressively increased. The battalion, during 1833-39, consisted of 1080 of all ranks organised into twelve companies. Of these as many as four companies or one-third of the battalion, was now composed of Gorkhas. These consisted of a variety of classes and a contemporary account listed as many as fourteen.[21] The same account says:

> The Gorkhas are a noble set of fellows distinguished by some of the virtues and stained also by a few of the vices peculiar to Europeans. Unlike the natives of Hindustan they do not yield themselves up to the demoralising custom of Assamese of taking large quantities of opium and maintaining on the establishment a plurality of women.

The Commanding Officer, Major Adam White's policy had been anxious to increase the Gorkha element and frequently sent recruiting parties to the Nepal frontier.

During the operations in the Khasi Hills a small irregular company called the Shah Militia was raised from Burmese prisoners of war settled in Singamari in 1825.[22] Another Sebundy corp was raised by the Agent to the Governor General Thomas Robertson in Gauhati in 1832 to take the place of two companies of regular troops under orders of withdrawal from the province. In October 1832 Captain Francis Jenkins and Lieutenant Robert Pemberton, in their report on Assam, had recommended the reorganisation of all the irregular companies into a single battalion. The report had recommended separate class companies with emphasis on local recruits. The proposal fell through when Robertson strongly objected to placing the irregulars under formal military control. In 1834-35 after he became Agent, Jenkins revised his earlier joint proposal. But his views on its composition underwent a change, for he now preferred the Rabhas of lower Assam.[23] The Governor General, Lord Bentinck who was concurrently the Commander-in-Chief since October 1832 gave his approval to the proposal and drew up elaborate guidelines for the reorganisation.[24] On this basis the Assam Sebundy corps was formed[25] out of the four existing Sebundy companies. The new corps was completed by drafts from the ALI[26] which was accordingly reduced by two companies. A significant difference between the Sebundy corps and the ALI was that the former was not entitled to pension or furlough.

Unlike Major White, the Governor General's Agent Captain Francis Jenkins was not favourably disposed towards the Gorkhas. He thought them to be less suitable than the Hindustanis for the North East Frontier. From their habits and way of life they suffered more from the effects of the climate and as soldiers did not strike him to be of the same superior class as the Hindustanis. He was, therefore, inclined to restrict recruiting in the ALI of this class of men. At any rate if Gorkhas were enlisted they were likely to become mixed up and assimilated with the upcountry sepoys. But for the remote frontier duties Jenkins was not prepared to employ the ALI and the Hindustanis for the unhealthiness of the climate; this apart, the battalion was intended to supply the place of a regular Bengal native infantry. From the time he assumed charge of the Agency in 1834 Jenkins, therefore, placed a good deal of emphasis on the recruitment of local tribes such as the Jarvas and Rabhas of Lower Assam or the Doanneahs* of the eastern districts and consequently the raising of the Sebundy regiments.

Further Changes

The local recruitment in the 2nd Assam Sebundy corps, however, ultimately failed. The Doanneahs and the border tribes belied the expectations of the Agent and the numbers were vastly reduced through discharges. Consequently, their further recruitment was stopped. In 1843 the class composition of the battalion was:[28]

Recruit from Upper Assam	—	148
Jarvas	—	340
Sylhetees and Manipuris	—	28
Hindustanis and Gorkhas	—	89

The Commanding Officer, Captain Phillip Mainwarring was keen on Gorkhas and Hindustanis and sought to improve the working conditions in the battalion to attract them. The corps though designated as a Sebundy was subjected to the same system of discipline and performed precisely the same duties as the local corps but were not entitled to the privilege of furlough. The sepoys discovering that a return to their home was absolutely barred during their service were disinclined to continue to service. Captain Mainwarring accordingly found it difficult to obtain any but inferior recruits of Upper Assam. In these circumstances he pleaded for the extension of furlough regulations to his battalion.

Meanwhile the 1st Assam Sebundy corps too had undergone a change in composition. Its Commandant, Captain Thomas Fisher was

* Men of mixed parentage of Singphos and Assamese.

disenchanted with his Jurwas just as Captain Mainwarring was with the Doanneahs. Within seven years, between 1835 and 1843, the number of discharges and desertions amounted to 224 or about one-third of the corps taken at its original number. Of these 105 have been discharged at their own request, 45 discharged for other causes, primarily as a result of Court Martial, and the remainder were desertions.[29] In this situation the Gorkhas and Hindustanis came to be recruited freely and had virtually become the backbone of the regiment. To attract the Gorkhas and Hindustani recruits, Captain Fisher agreed with Mainwarring that the furlough regulations should be extended to the Sebundies. This would, he pointed out, lead to the increased attachment to its service, maintain discipline and enable the officers to obtain Gorkhas and Hindustanis.

The Government of India impressed by these arguments agreed to grant furlough to the men of the Sebundy regiments. But a more important decision taken by the Government was the disbandment of the 2nd Sebundy corps. To implement this decision some of the Gorkhas and Hindustanis were transferred to the 1st battalion and others were absorbed in the local armed police establishment. In August 1844 the 1st Sebundies were upgraded into a light infantry battalion (local) and designated as the 2nd Assam Light Infantry, the senior corps being granted the title of 1st Battalion.[30] The two battalions were redistributed as follows:

1st ALI			2nd ALI		
Jaypur	...	4 Coys	Gauhati	...	4 Coys
Saikhowa	...	2 Coys	Tezpur	...	2 Coys
Tingral	...	1 Coy	Goalpara	...	2 Coys
Doom Dooma	...	1 Coy	Lakhimpur	...	1 Coy
Dibrugarh	...	2 Coys	Sibsagar	...	1 Coy

Each of the ALIs consisted of 1080 of all ranks organised into twelve companies.[31]

In the 2nd ALI the move towards the recruitment of Hindustanis and more particularly Gorkhas continued. The class composition in 1855 was this:

	Subadar	*Jemadar*	*Havildar*	*Naik*	*Bugler*	*Sepoy*	*Total*
Hindustani	1	3	6	5	1	162	177
Nepalese	1	1	5	7	1	95	110
Sylhetiahs	–	1	–	–	–	22	27
Bengalese	–	–	–	–	1	7	8
Jarvas	9	5	48	43	7	674	786
Manipuris	–	–	1	5	–	40	46

Captain Robert Campbell, Commandant of the 2nd ALI made an effort to improve the service conditions of the regiment. He solicited the re-establishment of 'Recruit Fund' which was abolished in 1848, with a view to obtaining new recruits and providing them with subsistence allowance, particularly the recruits from Nepal and North West Provinces.[32] He pleaded that subsistence allowance was necessary to avoid difficulties in obtaining new recruits as the amount had to be paid to the relatives of the recruits when first posted to the regiment as cost of supporting the recruits by them. This meant the re-establishment of the Extra Recruitment departial for the provision of 60 recruits at Rs. 2 per month.[33] Captain Campbell also advocated the attachment of a troop of cavalry to the regiment and the introduction of mini-rifles or rifle to fire the conical mini-bullets.

F.D. Atkinson, Military Secretary, in his letter to Jenkins supported the views of Captain Campbell in regard to the attachment of a troop of cavalry to the regiment and this apart, he recommended for the modification of the regiment by recruitment of two companies strength of Gorkhas, in addition to the Hindustanis.[34]

Police Militia: Their Composition

With the disbandment of the 2nd Sebundies and the upgradation of the 1st, the duties of the local corps once again extended to the defence of the frontier against the border tribes. The multiplication of the frontier outposts and the need for a disposable force for emergencies again led to the creation of irregular companies. Already such units had taken the duties of some of the frontier posts. In 1836 when Purander Singh's territory was resumed his 500 strong Pyke militia was reorganised into a smaller body of 100 men and redesignated the Assam Militia. It did not work well and was largely composed of the opium eating Assamese peasants. It was consequently reduced to fifty men when the Upper Assam Sebundy Corps was raised, but was again restored to its former strength, reorganised and better classes of men enlisted when the sebundies turned out to be numerically insufficient for the growing number of outposts. A small body of 120 men from the disbanded Sebundy Corps was at the same time retained for outposts and jail duties in Lakhimpur and formed the nucleus of the Lakhimpur Militia. In 1847 its strength was raised to 160. Likewise another group of ex-sebundies was detailed for the Angami-Naga frontier to act in concert with the Shan Militia which Jenkins had revived in 1840.

The relations with the hill tribes and security of the frontier which was never satisfactory deteriorated further from the middle of the 1840s. Against the Angamis, a series of expeditions began and local officers responsible for the defence of North Cachar and Nowgong began to pay more attention to the question of troops. Since the close of E.R. Granges' second expedition the security of the Angami-Naga frontier rested upon the Shah Militia and the ex-sebundies. Of the latter several were Gorkhas. Seeing their work Henry Bigge in 1840 had proposed raising two companies of Gorkhas but this did not find favour with the government.[35] Under his successor, John Butler Gorkhas and Hindustanis dominated the non-commissional ranks. Butler like Bigge did not consider the Shahs suitable, and at any rate these men had become very old. In 1845, after one of his numerous expeditions in the Angami Naga hills, Butler obtained the reluctant permission of the Agent to discharge the Shahs and recruit in their place local Dimasa Kacharis. He re-organised the company to one hundred men, introduced new scales of pay and uniforms on the model of the light infantry, and designated it as the Nowgong Police Militia. In 1851 after the tenth expedition its strength was raised to 150.

Meanwhile a new problem emerged in Cachar in the form of Lushai raids in the southern frontier. In February 1850 Colonel Frederick Lister urged that something decisive should be done against such raids.[36] He proposed to raise a two hundred strong militia from the Kukis who had been driven out by the Lushais. His proposal was immediately approved but as a measure of precaution the Government of India decided to restrict the Kuki element to only fifty per cent. The corps was organised into one British officer as Commandant, four tribal chiefs as Jemadars, ten Muntries as Havildars and 200 Kukis and Kacharis in equal proportion.[37] The corps came to be popularly known as the Kuki Levy. The success of the Kuki Levy induced Lieutenant H.S. Bivar in North Cachar in May 1854, to enlist twenty Angami youth into the Nowgong Police Militia.[38] The Secretary of the Foreign Department noted: "The Kookie levy has quite answered its purpose and there is no reason why a Naga levy should not do as well."[39] However, the Angamis did not remain long in service, for it appears that these independent tribes did not relish serving under the Hindustanis or Gorkha non-commissioned officers. Sir Alexander Mackenzie pointed out only eight months later about this fact.[40]

By the early months of 1820 it was clear that the local corps could no longer garrison numerous frontier outposts. The recurrence of the Burmese threat and Second Anglo-Burmese War (1852) re-emphasised the need to keep the local corps concentrated. Jenkin's solution to the problem was to increase the police militia. Under this instruction Captain Charles Holroyd, Sibsagar's magistrate reformed and reorganised the old Assam Militia, introduced better scales of pay to attract Gorkhas, replaced its old arms and redesignated it as the Sibsagar Police Militia.[41] Colonel Jenkins, at the same time, submitted detailed proposals for a 150 strong Garo Police Militia drawn from Garos, Rabhas and Hajongs for the defence of the Garo frontier. His plan was to have well organised police militia in Lakhimpur of 160 sepoys, in Sibsagar of 100, in Nowgong of 150 and in Goalpara 150 relieving the light infantry from unhealthy frontier outposts.[42] These plans, however, did not materialise. A.J. Moffat Mills, the Judge of the Sibsagar Diwani Adalat who was in Assam to enquire into the state of local administration considered it doubtful policy to increase the police militia for defence of frontiers. He would rather reduce the militia and entrust their duties of the frontier to local corps. A settlement of the question was further delayed as a result of the events of 1857-58.[43]

DEVELOPMENT OF GORKHA REGIMENTS

The early months of the mutiny of the Bengal army were of little anxiety to the Assam authorities for the local regiments continued to be loyal. The 1st ALI in June 1857 even volunteered for general service and a two hundred strong columns under the Second-in-Command was drawn up for service in the Upper Provinces. A military police battalion, the Kamroop Regiment was raised from tribes in lower Assam in the following month.[44] From August, however, the situation underwent a radical change. The defection of Raja Kunwar Singh of Jagdishpur soon sparked off a restlessness in the men of the 1st ALI in Upper Assam, particularly among those hailing from the Arrah district in Bihar. Already in Sibsagar and Golaghat districts a conspiracy was set on foot to seize power. However, a prompt action of arresting the ring leaders prevented further spread of the rebellion. In the Dibrugarh headquarters of the regiment precautionary measures were taken by its Commandant, Major Simon. The Gorkha companies were brought in from Sadiya and the Hindustanis dispensed to the outposts.[45] From contemporary accounts it is evident that it was the presence of the Gorkhas that instilled a sense of security in the European officers. A British sergeant of the regiment had recorded in his diary that "it seems that the presence of our Purbutteahs (hill or Gorkhas) have overawed the bad spirits in the corps and the station."[46]

Reorganisation

Although the development in Northern India did not have, on the whole a great impact upon the North East British Military Policy that resulted as a consequence was to have a more lasting effect. The Royal Commission on Army Reform in India under Major General Sir Jonathan Peel set-up to look into the whole question of the army in India and clearly laid down fundamental principles of reform. The large incidence of illness among Europeans and the hard military duties in India were other important reasons which made the recruitment of Indians unavoidable in considerable proportions. The problem then was how to make that army safe. The solution then was found in maintaining a large European army equipped with superior weapons as an effective counterpoise to Indian troops and also in the segregation of the three native armies and their organisation in such a manner as to set them caste against caste, religion against religion and company against company.[47] The Commission submitted its report in March 1859, in which it recommended *inter alia* an increase in the

British troops and a corresponding reduction in the Indian element maintaining 1 : 2 ratio between them; reorganisation of Indian armies in "different nationalities and castes and as a general rule, mixed promiscuously through each regiment" and the removal of arsenals and the artillery from Indian hands.[48]

An important decision that followed the report was the abolition of all irregular or paramilitary forces and the creation of uniform regiments on the lines laid down by the Commission. Accordingly in 1861, May, the Army Headquarters issued orders for delocalising the Assam corps and placing them in general roaster of the regular infantry regiments. The 1st and 2nd ALI became respectively the 46th and 47th (Assam) Native Infantry and SLI 48th (Sylhet) Infantry.[49] Its strength was fixed as in each Infantry regiments, at 600 men organised into 8 companies, each company composed of the following officers:[50]

1. Subadar : 5 Naiks
2. Jamadar : 2 Drummers
3. Havildars : 75 Privates

The five Gorkha battalions which were originally included in the General list of Bengal regiments were withdrawn from the line as per instructions of the Secretary of State for India and numbered separately from the 1st to the 4th—the Hazara Gurkha Battalion, attached to the Punjab Irregular Force being numbered the 5th. In the re-numbering of the regiments, that followed, the Assam and Sylhet battalions were re-designated, viz.[51]

42nd : Ist Assam Light Infantry Battalion
43rd : 2nd Assam Light Infantry Battalion
44th : Sylhet Light Infantry Battalion

Assam Battalions: Composition

As regular regiments of the Bengal army, the Sylhet and the Assam Light Infantry battalions came under the composition pattern laid down by the Peel Commission. There were four basic systems of mixed composition in the presidency armies. The "General Mixture" of "plum-pudding" system had been almost universe from the beginning in the Bombay and Madras armies. In Bengal the majority of the elder regiments were partially recruited and organised on this system. These men of different castes or classes mixed together in the companies, however, no fixed rules as to the proportion of each class was fixed. The advocates of this system held that mixture of castes in a single regiment was a good method of ending the pretensions of superiority of the higher classes. Under this system they would be brought on the same level with the low caste men in drill, guards and other military duties. Under the class company system the men belonging to different classes were organised into separate companies. In Bengal, a large number of regiments were of this class company system after the mutiny. These were drawn wholly from one district, caste or class, such as the Gorkhas and Sikhs. An extreme variation of this was the village system where regiments were composed of men drawn from a single village.[52]

At the time of re-organisation the Sylhet and the Assam Light Infantry were, by and large, of a heterogeneous character. A variety of men over the years had been enlisted though these were generally kept in separate companies. In June 1859, the 1st ALI had, for example, the following composition:

Hindustanis	:	600
Gorkhas	:	250
Manipuris, Jarvas etc.	:	260

The battalion fell under the category of "General Mixture",[53] that is having an indiscriminate mixture of companies. The Government of India did not, however, consider it necessary to lay down specific rules as to the proportion of each class to be enlisted. These corps being intended principally for service in North Eastern India should ordinarily recruit from the neighbouring localities and particularly from hill men. But it was emphasised that the Hindustani element should be restricted to one-fourth of the strength of each regiment.[54]

Reduction: Shower's Report

Reduction in the regiment began from 1861. Their strength before the new regulations came into effect was:[55]

		Headquarters
Ist ALI (42nd)	1000	Dibrugarh
2nd ALI (43rd)	1000	Gauhati
SLI (44th)	1200	Sylhet

These regiments were now drastically reduced in strength, the first two by four hundred men each and the third by six hundred. The total reduction in the provincial garrison amounted to fourteen hundred men. Since, the regiment had a number of outposts under their commanding officers began to complain that reduction to new level could be carried out only if they were relieved of their frontier outpost duties.[56] The army authorities saw little difficulty in this since they considered outpost duties as purely police duties.[57] But the police militia which had been raised to relieve the local corps from the outposts had meanwhile been abolished on the recommendations of the Police Commission of 1860. In their place a constabulary was organised as Civil Police and outpost duties were now interpreted as a military function.

In these circumstances John Peter Grant, the Lieutenant Governor of Bengal found sufficient grounds to take up the question of the number of troops required in the North East Frontier. After consulting the local authorities particularly Henry Hopkinson, who had meanwhile succeeded Colonel Francis Jenkins as Agent to the Governor General, Grant in January 1862 placed his requirements before the Governors General-in-Council as follows: five regiments of native infantry, a few companies of Europeans, both infantry and artillery, he said was "absolutely necessary". The Government of India was not prepared to concede to the Lieutenant Governor's demands but since he and his local officers made repeated representations for additional regiments they decided to depute a senior military officer to the North East to report upon its defences. As Brigadier General S.G.D. Showers, GOC Presidency Division, who was asked to proceed to Assam for the purpose was on his way, in the early part of 1862, news reached him of his appointment as Commissioner of the Khasi and Jaintia Hills.

The Jaintia uprising which began in January, the second in two years, was getting out of hand and Showers task was its immediate suppression. The 44th regiment which moved in from Cherrapunjee at its reduced strength under the Command of Lieutenant Colonel William Richardson was found to be inadequte[58] and Showers, therefore, induced two additional regiments one Hindustani and one Sikh. After two months of experience of the Jaintia insurrection General Showers was convinced that the permanent garrison for the North East should not be less than five full regiments. In the lengthy report submitted in September 1862.[59] Showers recommended:

Bishnath	:	½ Regiment Native Infantry and 3 Companies of Europeans
Gauhati	:	1 Regiment, Native Infantry
Dhubri	:	½ Regiment, Native Infantry
Cherapunjee	:	1 Regiment, Native Infantry
Jowai	:	1 Regiment, Native Infantry
Dibrugarh	:	1 Regiment, Native Infantry, 1 Company local Artillery

Showers disagreed that regiments of Hindustanis, men of the lower provinces and even the Sikhs were not as suited for the North East Frontier as the Gorkhas and local recruits. While recommending their employment the GOC, however, clearly laid down the importance of periodic reliefs. The old Assam regiments, the 42nd, the 43rd and the 44th should, therefore, be effectively delocalised and occasionally posted out of the region.

The local officers in Assam were, however, not prepared to see the local regiments relieved by other Bengal regiments. The former had contained a large element of Gorkhas and local soldiers who, it was feared, would seek discharge if their regiments were posted out of the provinces. And it was considered important to retain their services since they were "the best suited for the petty border-warfare" in the North East.[60] The Government of Bengal accordingly decided to keep these regiments as near the region as possible. With this exception Showers report in its essentials was approved in 1864. A Brigadier General was appointed and the North East became a separate military command styled the Eastern Frontier District.

Policy Re-examined

The composition of the regiments shortly afterwards came to be re-examined. The Anglo-Bhutan War (1864-65) had exposed the inefficiency of the 43rd regiment. The regiment commanded by Lieutenant Colonel Campbell had not only failed to hold Dewangiri, an important post in the frontier, during the first place of the operations against the Bhutanese, but a hasty retreat from the place had ended in a complete rout. A Military Court of Enquiry into the disaster recorded in March 1865 its opinion that this was due, *inter alia,* to the inferior class of men composing the regiment.[61] In his review of the report Sir William Mansfield, Bengal's Commander-in-Chief, had observed that although a certain proportion of the regiment were trustworthy, referring to the Gorkhas and Hindustanis, there was a number of Assamese peasants who were not of the fighting classes. They were said to be great opium eaters and totally unfit as soldiers. He, therefore, decided to replace these men, some 337 of all ranks by Gorkhas and Hindustanis best suited for service in Assam. The regiment was accordingly withdrawn from the scene of operation[62] to Gauhati so that its reorganisation could be carried under the direct supervision of the Brigadier General commanding the Eastern Frontier.

More specific proposals were submitted by Brigadier General Sir Henry Tombs, who had commanded the Right column of the Doar (Bhutan) Field Force. Tombs' scheme consisted of the organisation of the military in Assam into two columns, one based in Dibrugarh and the other in Goalpara for full service at a moment's notice. Each of these columns should consist of half a company of Sappers and Miners, a Mountain Train Battery, half a British Regiment, wing of Cavalry and two native infantry regiments, one Gorkha and the other Pathan and Sikh. The proposal did not find favour either with the Government of India or with the military authorities.

Meanwhile reports had been received that the Hindustanis regiments in the Khasi Hills were suffering from the effects of the climate[63] and the Bengal Government were now asking for suitable native troops for garrison duties in the hills. In July 1865, Sir William Mansfield accordingly submitted a plan for the formation of two local regiments.[64] He felt that the proper model for such troops were the Gorkha regiments of the Bengal Presidency and the Sind regiment of that of Bombay who had always displayed greater fighting qualities than the Hindustani regiments. What was required on the North East Frontier, he said, where men who could grapple with the hill tribes on their own grounds, men who were individually courageous and stout and who were not entirely dependant on training. On these grounds Mansfield felt that two regiments should be exclusively raised from local service on the North East Frontier. They should be drawn from the Gorkhas, particularly from Eastern Nepal and Sikkim. One-fourth should be reserved for the frontier tribes to be mixed up with Gorkhas. The Headquarters of one of the regiments was to be fixed at Shillong. It was also proposed that these two local regiments with the 42nd, 43rd and 44th Regiments properly organised would be sufficient for the military occupation and defence of the North East Frontier.

This proposal of the Commander-in-Chief with that of General Tombs did not meet with the approval of the Government of India. Instead, the Governor General-in-Council suggested that the 42nd, 43rd and 44th Regiments should be made efficient by weeding out unfit men, and was prepared to sanction an increase of two or three hundred men to each of them. The 44th SLI already overburdened in the Khasi Hills was allowed to be augmented to eight hundred men,[65] followed shortly thereafter by the 42nd, 43rd Regiments. In December of 1865 after the augmentation was complete the Commander-in-Chief withdrew one regiment of Native Infantry and re-distributed the garrison as follows:[66]

Dibrugarh (H.Q.)	: 42nd Regiment
Tezpur	: Native Local Artillery
Gauhati (H.Q.)	: 43rd Regiment
Cherrapunjee (H.Q.)	: 44th Regiment
Cachar and outposts	: Wing of the 5th Regiment Native Infantry

Class Regiment: Gradual Shift

Meanwhile within the regiments a good deal of discussion had been taking place regarding their composition. In the 42nd Sikhs and

Hindustanis continued to be enlisted and its Commanding Officer Colonel Thomas Rattray was keen to organise his battalion under the class company system. At his earnest recommendation the Government of India agreed in December 1868 to the following organisation:[67]

Sikhs	...	2 Companies
Gorkhas	...	4 Companies (with 25% Jarvas in each)
Hindustanis	...	2 Companies (one Hindu and one Mussalman)

Rattray's own preference was for the Sikhs and he sent Lieutenant J.W. Alexander to the Punjab to recruit these companies. Rattray in fact wanted to convert this regiment into a Sikh one and it is said that it was the united oppositions of his officers, particularly Captain William Brydon and William Abbot, that prevented him from eliminating the Gorkhas completely.[68] But the impetus to further recruitment of Gorkhas actually came from the GOC, Eastern Frontier District, Sir William Fraser Tytler. General Tytler was apparently a great admirer of the Gorkhas and correspondingly less attracted to the Sikhs or Hindustanis. His views are best recorded by Colonel Hopkinson.[69]

> I was present myself on one occasion at a conversation between ....(the) Brigadier General and a Commanding Officer whose Nepalese (Gorkhas) were at that time drawn as rice eaters. The General wanted more Nepalese enlisted; wanted in fact as I understood him, the regiment to be Gorkha. The Commanding Officer objected that the pay was not high enough to be attractive and was then told to calculate his compensation as for *atta*.

Hopkinson was alluding to compensation for dearness of provisions. Men who subsisted on *atta* or wheat flour was granted an additional allowance as compensation since that commodity not locally available was expensive. The following table shows the actual compensation of all ranks during 1867-68:[27]

Recruiting Ground		*Number*
Punjab	...	246
Oudh	...	5
Nepal	...	269
Bihar	...	280
Assam (Jarvas)	...	105
Total	**...**	**905**

Of those the last three, and particularly those from Nepal were rice eaters and only the first two were *atta* eaters and all were paid the extra allowance. The GOC had hoped that this would be a sufficient inducement to attract the Gorkhas.

Thereafter, recruitment of Gorkhas into three regiments increased. As a result of representations from the majority of the commandants and other officers the Government of India issued orders in June 1871 to remove the Hindustanis from the regiment filling their vacancies with Gorkhas.[71] In the 42nd, however, permission was granted to enlist relations of the Sikhs and Hindustanis[72] for some time longer.

Gorkha Light Infantry

The Frontier wars of the decade fully established the relevance of Gorkhas in the North East Frontier. Their recruitment had as a result increased. During 1878-79 recruits were obtained from the Darjeeling district and from 1880 advantage was taken of the depot at Gorakhpur.[72] By this time the 44th had virtually become a first class Gorkha regiment. So, highly expressed were the military authorities of its fighting qualities that the regiment was ordered in early 1879 to the North West Frontier for field service.[73]

In 1881, the Government of India issued orders in supersession of all previous orders on the subject, restricting the enlistment of all classes of Gorkhas to the purely Gorkha battalions, and the 42nd, 43rd and 44th Regiments of Native Infantry. Under the Government of India Orders, the word "Native" was eliminated from the designations of all regiments of native Infantry. Thus, Bengal Native Infantry became "Bengal Infantry" and so on. The titles in January

1885, were 44th Regiment (SLI) (Light Infantry) and 43rd Regiment (ALI). By January 1886, (Light Infantry) portion of the 44th title was dropped. In June 1886, the titles were once more changed to 44th Regiment Gurkha (Light) Infantry and 43rd Regiment Gurkha (Light) Infantry and on the formation of a schemes of reserves (the same year) the two Regiments were linked with the 42nd Gurkha Light Infantry the present 6th Gurkha Rifles.[74] For some reasons unknown the 43rd continued the spelling "Goorkha" as against the "Gurkha" of the other two regiments.

On 1 January, 1877, a grand parade of all arms was held at Delhi at which Her Majesty Queen Victoria was proclaimed Empress of India. This was the first of the proclamation parades held in India in every military station.

MILITARY POLICE

The development of the old Sylhet and Assam regiments into first rate Gorkha corps would not have been possible but for the organisation of the frontier police by which it was relieved of much of the distressing duties of the frontier. The police militia, it will be recalled, were abolished under the Police Act V of 1861 and the units absorbed into the new police constabulary.[75] These functioned as the armed branch and from 1866 gradually relieved the troops at the outposts. Since then and until 1874 when Assam was constituted into a Chief Commissionership the Bengal Government made several attempts to improve their efficiency. In 1868 a proposal was made to separate the armed branch from the civil constabulary reconstituting it as a frontier police.[76] The Government of India was, however, unwilling to take up schemes involving additional outlay at the time of great financial difficulties. The proposal was revived by Edward Baker, Deputy Inspector General of Police, Assam Circle in 1873. Baker had recommended that the police in the frontier districts of Assam, should be divided into civil and frontier establishments, the latter to take all guard, outpost escort and quasi-military duty of every kind. The Lieutenant Governor thought that the schemes were particularly appropriate to the Assam Frontier and forwarded it with its strongest recommendation to the Government of India.[77] Once again the proposal fell through, this time mainly because a Chief Commissioner was about to take over Assam and the matter was best left for his consideration. The problem of a newly constituted province left little time for Colonel Richard Keating, Assam's first Chief Commissioner to turn his attention fully to the police and it was not before another four years when the subject was again taken up.

In 1878, in consequence of disturbances in the Angami-Naga Hills, briefly noticed earlier an addition of 300 men to the frontier police of Assam, for the Naga Hills, had been sanctioned.[78] The Government of India at the same time approved the separation of the Assam Police into two distinct branches of armed and unarmed force of the following strength:[79]

	Armed or Frontier Police	*Unarmed Police*
Inspector	8	20
Sub-Inspectors	30	57
Head Constables	195	176
Constables	1,941	1230
Total	**2,174**	**1,483**
Grand Total = 3,657		

The armed or frontier police was to perform the duties of the Sadar jail and treasury guards, of escorts, and the garrisoning of the numerous frontier outposts. The unarmed or civil police were to be entrusted with the work ordinarily performed by the police station, the Sadar and sub-divisional courts.

Military Police

The suitability of the police for the ordinary frontier work was by now more fully appreciated. They cost much less than the military—Rs. 180 per constable against Rs. 337 per sepoy, per annum—was more easily mobilised being able to move out in a moment's notice without transport or commissariat arrangements. Above all the health of the men suffered less from the effects of the climate. A definite recruitment Policy had not yet evolved and the men were "enlisted for their qualities as soldiers from among such races as the Nepalese or tribes inhabiting the hills, and slopes of Assam such as Jarvas, Rabhas, Cacharis." In August 1879 Sir Stewart Bayley who had in the meanwhile succeeded Colonel Keating as Chief Commissioner, therefore, proposed its response to an enquiry by the Eden Commission, then enquiring into the Army in India, to reduce the military garrison and increase the frontier police. The main proposals as summed up by Bayley were:"[80]

(1) to relive the military of all frontier outposts duty.
(2) to make this duty over to the frontier police.
(3) bring up the strength of the frontier police to 3000 men.
(4) to reduce the military garrison of Assam by two regiments.

The Army Commission guided by the opinions of General Frederick Roberts and Colonel Charles MacGregor both of whom had experience of frontier expeditions on the North East, decided not to recommend the reduction of the garrison fully down to the Chief Commissioner's proposal.[81] But they fully agreed that duties of the frontier posts in Assam was more work of the police than the army. The problem remained in obeyance for 2 years until in January 1882, the Commander-in-Chief Sir Donald Stewart proposed not only to relieve the troops from outpost duties but also to improve the quality of the frontier police. The duties of the latter he recognised were more military than of a civil nature. The following year Assam's new Chief Commissioner Sir Charles Elliot further elaborated upon these proposals.[82] These, which the Government of India approved in 1883-84, were:

(1) Constitution of territorially four divisions of frontier police.
(2) Relief of troops from outposts duties by frontier police.
(3) Relief of frontier police from station duties by Civil police.

By 1884-85 the reorganised frontier police was well in operation. The Assam Frontier Police was now organised into four battalions and two independent detachments, viz.,

	Subadar	*Jemadar*	*Havildar*	*Sipahi*
Surma Valley Battalion	3	14	73	712
Lakhimpur	2	8	58	614
Naga Hills	4	9	43	502
Garo Hills	2	6	24	302
Darrang Detachment	—	1	6	60
Sibsagar	—	2	10	120
Total	**11**	**40**	**214**	**2310**

Further, change in organisation soon followed. In 1889 introduction of Civil Police in the Garo and Naga Hills Districts led to a reduction in the strength of those battalions. However, in case of Naga Hills District the decrease was counter-balanced by the addition of the Mokokchung sub-division. At the same time, the Sibsagar Detachment was also reduced as a consequence of the increase in the Sibsagar civil armed police. This was amalgamated with the Lakhimpur Battalion although the outpost in that district continued to be maintained for some years. By 1890 the strength of the battalions of all ranks stood at—[83]

Surma Valley Battalion	...	792
Lakhimpur Battalion	...	752
Naga Hills Battalion	...	671
Garo Hills Battalion	...	243
Darrang Detachment	...	67

Recruitment Problems

Until the reforms initiated by Sir Charles Elliot no definite recruitment pattern was adopted for the military police. The old militia and frontier police recruited men as they came and in each district a good number of Gorkhas had been taken in. In 1882 as part of the reforms Elliot had recommended that of the number of recruits enlisted annually, fifty per cent should be chosen from Gorkhas and the rest from Jarvas and Kacharis. "We cannot get for the police quite as good a class of Goorkhas as the military can obtain," the Chief Commissioner had said, "but I am informed that we have for the last two or three years succeeded in enlisting a very fair number of Nepalese of good physique and fighting tradition."[84]

With only vacancies to be filled the Chief Commissioner's annual requirement of Gorkhas was by no means a large one. Yet considerable difficulty was experienced even for this small number. It was a time when British demands for these men were as high as it was difficult to persuade the Nepal Durbar to permit enlistment of their subjects into the Indian army. Until his death in 1877 Jang Bahadur Rana stood firmly opposed to recruit his Gorkhas and the methods adopted by the British to obtain them has been well brought out in a recent study:[85]

> There was no regular arrangement with the Nepalese Government for the supply of recruits. The Nepalese Government in fact never willingly allowed their men to take British service because it drained off Nepal's own strength and made the British proportionality strong. In such circumstances recruitment had to be done *sub rosa* recruitment agents being sent out surreptitiously into the Nepalese territory. Oftener, at fairs in the border towns and villages quite few men were obtained. Gurkhas of the Indian army on leave in Nepal also managed to smuggle out some men and were rewarded by the Government.

The situation did improve under Jang Bahadur's successors and the army had enough problems in keeping the Gorkha corps up to their full strength. During the Afghan war when the military authorities were pressing for addition to the regiments by a thousand men an attempt was made through the Nepal Durbar. This failed when after six months of persuasion and an expenditure of ten thousand rupees only 559 were obtained of whom 393 were found unfit—"the lame, the halt, the maimed and the blind". Since, the Durbar could not be relied upon to supply recruits commandants of Gorkha corps had been urging the Government of India to that unless recruiting parties were allowed inside Nepal or a depot established in Kathmandu itself no good men would be obtainable. Political considerations ruled out such a course but in the new a few good deal of discussions took place between senior military officers and the Government of India on the best means of inducing the corporation of the reluctant Nepal Durbar.[86] But Nepal remained unmoved and in early 1883 the Government of India by a General Order restricted the enlistment of Gorkhas into the purely Gorkha corps and the 42nd, 43rd and 44th regiments in Assam.[87] The Assam Authorities, therefore, had to rely on whatever material were available locally for the military police. The best classes were no longer available and the percentage of Gorkha fell from 50 to 42. Recruitment of Jarvas increased and in some battalions even Dogras were enlisted.[88]

The army's problems became acute towards 1885 in the face of the Russian difficulty in Central Asia.[89] Plans were immediately laid to add a second battalion to each of the five Gorkha regiments for which no less than 5600 men were required. Nepal faced with a crisis with Tibet[90] and in need of modern weapons finally agreed to cooperate and an agreement was struck. The result was that for the first time recruitment of Gorkhas became more systematic. Gorakhpur, for years the rendezvous for recruiting parties now became a recruitment depot under a British officer. But Assam's difficulties were by no means over. The terms of service offered by the Burma military police, raised after the annexation of Upper Burma in 1885-86, were more attractive heading to numerous desertions in the Assam battalions, the men supply crossing the frontier to enlist in Burma. The problem was only partly solved by making in 1886, the terms of the Assam service equally popular by such concessions as ground or free passage home on furlough. Assam had problems with the quality of men too.

With the great exponent of the "martial races" theory[91] Lord Roberts as Commander-in-Chief since 1885 the army began to claim exclusive rights over the Magars and Gurungs of Central and Western Nepal and were not prepared to let police battalions enlist from this class. Gorakhpur now became the depot solely for the army and a new depot in Purnia (and subsequently in Ghoom in Darjeeling) was established for the police battalions. Men from eastern Nepal, primarily Limbus and Rais, were thus made available for the police through the Purnia Depot. In early 1888 however, Sir William Word, Assam's Chief Commissioner sought permission to recruit from Gorakhpur none other than Magars and Gurungs reserved for the army. Word answered the military authorities that his recruiting parties would produce the Gorkhas before the officer-in-charge in Gorakhpur to verify that the marital tribes were not being taken for the police. It took some time to convince the Government of India and it was not before 1890 when the new arrangement was approved.

Assam nevertheless continued to enlist Magars and Gurungs from the Purnia Depot. The following figures of recruitment in the Purnia Depot during 1892-93 makes interesting reading.[92]

	Total	*For Army*	*For Police*
Limbus	87	67	20
Rais	103	48	55
Magars	66	3	63
Gurungs	65	6	59
Khas	46	2	44
Damais	12	5	7
Others	124	—	124
	503	**131**	**372**

The Army was recruiting more eastern than the police whose intake of the "reserved" Magars and Gurungs far exceeded that of the former. With Lord Roberts trying to replace by 2,500 Gorkhas an equal number of Madras and Bombay troops.[93] The military authorities saw no reason why Assam should recruit from Gorakhpur. In June 1893 the Government of India accordingly decided that Assam should no longer recruit their men from Gorakhpur. In the following year recruiting parties from Assam were stopped in Gorakhpur. The officer-in-charge of the depot justifying his action on the ground that he had received orders to the effect that the Assam Military Police were prohibited from recruiting Gorkhas there and were only entitled to the depot in Purnia and Darjeeling. The Chief Commissioner at once protested pointed out that the recruits obtained from Eastern Nepal were inferior in morale and physique.[94] It would, therefore, be detrimental to the efficiency of the military police if permission to recruit in Gorakhpur was withdrawn. Word also drew the attention of the Government of India to their approval in 1890 to Assam recruiting from Gorakhpur and that he found that there were no records rescinding this order.

Meanwhile relations with Nepal began to improve since Lord Roberts celebrated visit to Kathmandu in March 1892. Nepalese Prime Minister Bir Samsher was won over by presents of Martini-Henry Rifles and 7 pounder-field guns and a KCSI.[95] As a result of this, recruits from Nepal were for the first time more readily available. The Military Department, therefore, decided to withdraw the restriction placed on recruitment of Magars and Gurungs of Eastern Nepal for the military police. These, however, were to be obtained through the recruiting officer-in-charge of the Purnia Depot. From Gorakhpur only men from Eastern Nepal were permitted for enlistment.

Expansion

The ease with which Gorkhas were now available made possible the organisation of the Lushai Hills Military Police Battalion. After the conclusion of the Third Anglo Burmese War it was decided to establish control over the Lushai Hills in order to put a stop to the raids by Lushais in the plains of Cachar and Chittagong hill tracts. A series of mılıtary expeditions brought these hills as well as the Chin Hills of Burna under effective military domination. Since 1890, the whole of Surma Valley Battalion had been transferred to the North Lushai Hills, then under the Assam administration. In 1893, as a result of the decision to permanently occupy the Lushai Hills the Headquarters of the Battalion was moved from Silchar to Aijal, its name being changed to North Lushai Hills Battalion. The South Lushai Hills were at this time administered by Bengal and it maintained a battalion of military police at Lungleh.[96] This was the South Lushai Hills Military Police which grew out of the old frontier police of the Chittagong Hill tracts. In 1898 the whole of the Lushai Hill district was transferred to Assam and the North and South Lushai Hills Battalions were amalgamated into a single battalion of ten companies with the headquarters at Aijal under the name Lushai Hills Military Police. The Assam Military Police now stood as follows:[97]

Lushai Hills Battalion	...	970
Lakhimpur Battalion	...	848
Naga Hills Battalion	...	672

Silchar Detachment	...	372
Garo Hills Detachment	...	202

The two detachments were subsequently abolished and absorbed into the other two battalions. The Lushai Hills quickly settled down and with the introduction of civil police the work of the military police was reduced. In 1909 the Battalion was accordingly reduced from ten to eight companies.

The organisation of the Military Police Battalion remained unchanged until the creation in 1905 of the Eastern Bengal and Assam province. A small company of seventy six men was stationed in Dacca. The Swadeshi movement following the Partition added a new dimension to the problem of internal security of Eastern Bengal. As a result it became necessary to reinforce the Dacca Company with a detachment from Silchar. In addition detachment from the Lushai Hills Battalion from Lakhimpur, the Garo Hills and the Naga Hills were also inducted. An intelligence report of 1908 does point out the importance of locating Gorkhas in Dacca.[98]

> A regiment of regulars if located permanently at Dacca would, in consequence of the climate and the absence of amenities, soon go to pieces, nor would any regular regiments other than Gurkha Military Police. The people do not know the difference between regulars and military police, whereas they have already learnt to entertain a very lively respect for the Gurkha ... I do not think the Gurkha military police can be improved upon as an agency for producing moral effect and doing effecting service of the kind likely to be necessary in Eastern Bengal and Assam, and if any increase is required, it might be in this force....Indian revolutionary literature indicate that any display of force against Government (if indulged in) will be of the guerilla order, and that being so, can be best dealt with by armed police reserves and military police. I advocate the retention of two regular battalions in addition, not so much for the moral effect to be produced, but as a reserve which the present political situation would point to as necessary.

Meanwhile important changes were being carried out in the military commands in India. In 1905, Lord Kitchener's Scheme of military reorganisation and redistribution came into effect.[99] The principle underlying it was that the army in peace should be organised and trained in units of command similar to those in which who will take the field. The regiments in Assam were placed under the Eighth (Lucknow) Division. As part of his reorganisation scheme the three Gorkha regiments in Assam underwent change of designation. The 42nd Regiment had already become in 1901 the 42nd Gurkha Rifles and in 1903 when the Gorkha corps were brigaded became the 6th Gurkha Rifles. The 44th became the 8th Gurkha Rifles in 1903 and in 1907 became its first battalion. The 43rd which in 1903 was the 7th Gurkha Rifles became in 1907 the Second Battalion 8th Gurkha Rifles. With these regiments now forming part of Gorkha Brigade their services were not utilised elsewhere and more particularly in the North West Frontier. As a result addition and reorganisation in the Military Police became a necessity.

In 1910 the whole Military Police of Eastern Bengal and Assam was reorganised. The Lakhimpur Battalion was reduced by one company and the Dacca, Silchar and Garo Hills detachments were amalgamated into one battalion with Headquarters at Dacca. The sanctioned strength of the reorganised force was:[100]

Lushai Hills Battalion	...	850
Lakhimpur Battalion	...	673
Naga Hills Battalion	...	704
Dacca Battalion	...	784

Reorganisation: Early Reforms

Since 1910, the situation in the northern frontier of Assam underwent a rapid change. Taking advantage of the development following the Young Husband's expedition (and Lhasa Convention 1904) China quickly proceeded to establish her military control over Tibet. In early 1910 the Chinese army under Chao Erh-fang overran the eastern region and by the close of the year occupied Lhasa. The Dalai Lama fled to India. Chinese penetration into the tribal areas of what is now Arunachal Pradesh commenced at the same time. In May that year

Rima beyond the Mishmi Hills was occupied and a tribal chief was ordered "to cut a track from Tibet to Assam brought enough for two horsemen to ride abreast." This was followed by the Chinese hoisting a flag at Walong, several miles within Mishmi territory. Until the murder of the Assistant Political Officer of Sadiya, Nowell Williamson, and a tea garden doctor by the Abor tribes the Government of India had ignored the local governments persistent appeals for a more active frontier policy. The expedition against the Abors to avenge the murders and the subsequent exploratory missions resulted in opening of the frontier by lines of communication and also of setting up of two administrative units, the Sadiya and Balipara frontier tracts under a system of "loose political control". Earlier at the Simla Conference (1913-14) the northern limits of the tract was determined along the crest of the main Himalayan range, commonly known as the McMohan Line.[101]

In the meanwhile the Partition of Bengal had been undone and Assam reverted to a Chief Commissionership. In 1913 the Chief Commissioner submitted a proposal to the Government of India to raise a fourth military police battalion with a view to meeting the new responsibilities in the northern frontier of Assam. Earl took advantage of his proposal to suggest a uniform organisation of the military police battalions of eight companies of 704 sepoys or 800 of all ranks. The strength of the battalion and the companies had so long varied and considerable difficulty was being experienced in this regard. When for example the Inspector General detailed the company for any duty he could not do so without making enquiries of the number of rifles that would be furnished and it was frequently necessary to make up the numbers of units required by temporary transfer from other units. But Earl's most important recommendation was the restructuring of the class composition of the battalions. His recommendation were:[102]

Gorkhas	4 Companies	=	50 per cent
Jarvas	2 Companies	=	25 per cent
Dogras	2 Companies	=	25 per cent
Total	**8 Companies**	**=**	**100 per cent**

The Chief Commissioner was only too aware of the difficulties of a total dependence on Nepal to supply recruits. His scheme involved the reduction of some 300 Gorkhas and an addition of 350 Jarvas and 770 Dogras.

Army headquarters welcomed the proposal and the Adjutant General's Branch noted:[103]

> The proposed reduction of Gurkhas is desirable and is accepted. There is no objection to the increased enlistment of Jarvas nor to Dogras being enlisted up to the number proposed, provided only Jat and Brahman Dogras are taken. There is a good and plentiful supply of the former available, as they are little enlisted in the Indian Army. Experience has shown that they (Dogra Jats) do not mix well with Dogra Rajputs although when kept in companies by themselves with their Non-Commissioned officer they do excellently.
>
> While the proposed class composition of 50 per cent Gurkhas, 25 per cent Dogras and 25 per cent Jarvas is concurred in, with the above restriction as to Dogras, the attention of the Assam Government may be invited to the possibility of enlisting Bhutias who at present are not enlisted in the Indian Army but who might form a valuable addition to the Assam Military Police Force.

These proposals were approved in 1915 and recruitment for the new battalion commenced almost immediately. An interesting feature of these reforms related to the question of armaments. The Assam Government had urged the re-arming of the whole of the Assam Military Police with 303 Rifles. Assam had argued that owing to the increased responsibilities for border security thrown upon the Military Police the Martini-Henry Rifle was an insufficient arm. Despite persuasion from the Home Department the Government of India advised by the military authorities to turn this down. The Martini-Henry Rifle was rather too long for the short statured Gorkhas and to make it more convenient to the Gorkhas the bayonets were shortened by several inches.[104]

The outbreak of the First World War intervened the reorganisation process. The new frontier battalion still incomplete, was transferred to Manipur to relieve the 123 out from rifles. The War also made enormous demands for men to fill in vacancies in the Gorkha

Regiments and from 1915-16 the Military Police was required to send drafts to the regular armies. By early February 1917, 2788 officers and men were supplied and by January 1918, altogether 3162 drafts had been despatched.[105] Urgent demands upon the military police in view over extensive operations against the Kukis in Manipur had made it necessary to suspend sending Gorkhas to the regular army. As a result of these demands the strength of the battalions were raised to 1000 of all ranks. By early 1919, the men returned from the regular army.

RECRUITMENT POLICY 1919-20

An important result of the cooperation in the great war of Gorkhas of the Assam Military Police with the regular army was the permanent affiliation of the force to the Gorkha Rifles. Another and more far reaching was the re-designation in 1918 of the force as the Assam Rifles.[105] The Lushai Hills Battalion became the 1st Assam Rifles, the Lakhimpur the 2nd, the Naga Hills Battalion as the 3rd and the fourth in Manipur as the 4th Assam Rifles. In the following year Assam's Chief Commissioner Sir Nicholas Beatson Bell not only re-raised the frontier battalion but carried out important changes in the class composition of the battalions. With the transfer of the new battalion to Manipur the Lakhimpur battalion was inadequate for the Balipara and Sadiya frontier tracts. Besides a large number of Gorkhas drafted into the Gorkha corps had now returned following the end of the war. Bell had at the same time introduced the platoon system in place of the old Company system. During the war the Dogras were unobtainable and the new battalion had been recruited entirely from Gorkhas and Jarvas. The other battalions too were composed of most exclusively of these two classes. The Chief Commissioner considered both as excellent. But did not think "it right that Assam should depend so largely on Nepal for its garrison when it had so much promising material in its own hills." He accordingly approved the recruitment of Lushais for the 1st battalion, Nagas for the third and Kukis for the fourth battalion. He began by enlisting hundred men of "local levies" in each of these battalions, hoping that if the experiment was a success the Assam Rifles may eventually become practically self-supporting. He at the same time raised a number of men from Assam in each battalion to three hundred. It was not practicable to enlist any of the tribes from the two frontier tracts and Sir Nicholas Bell, therefore, decided that failing Dogras the composition of the second (Sadiya) and the fifth (Balipara) battalions should be Gorkhas 500 and Assamese 300. He still hoped that some of the tribes, Bhutanese, Akas, Daflas, Mishmis etc., may be found suitable later.

Bell's experiments were not without success and laid the foundation of class composition of the Assam Rifles. When the Assam Rifles Manual was prepared the ideal class composition was fixed as,[107]

1st (Lushais Hills) Battalion

50 %	Gurkhas
37 ½ %	Jarvas, Cacharis, Assamese
12 %	Lushais

2nd (Lakhimpur) Battalion

62 ½ %	Gurkhas
37 ½ %	Jarvas, Cacharis, Ahoms and other Assamese

3rd (Naga Hills) Battalion

50 %	Gurkhas
37 ½ %	Jarvas, Cacharis, Ahoms and other Assamese
12 ½ %	Nagas (Semas and Angamis)

4th Battalion

50 %	Gurkhas.
37 ½ %	Jarvas, Ahoms and other Assamese
12 ½ %	Kukis

5th Battalion

50 %	Gurkhas
50 %	Jarvas, Cacharis, Ahoms and other Assamese.

This remained unchanged till the British left in 1947.

NOTES

1. H.H. Wilson: *Documents Illustrative of the Burmese War* (Calcutta 1827) No. 24, also A.C. Banerjee, *The Eastern Frontier of British India:* (Calcutta 1964), Chap. VII, pp. 200-245.
2. FSC 26 November, 1824: No. 11, Scott to Swinton, 9 November.
3. F.G. Cardew: *A Sketch of the Services of the Bengal Native Infantry* (Calcutta 1903) pp. 139.

4. F.P.C. 9 August, 1822; No. 56. The Cuttack Legion was raised in May 1817 by Capt. Simon Fraser. The existing Rangpur Battalion was redesignated as the Dinajpur Local Battalion.
5. FSC 19 March, 1824: No. 64, 19 February, 1824. The Rangpur and SLC was converted into Light Infantry in the course of the year. See also Col. H.J. Huxford, *History of 8th Gorkha Rifles 1824-47* (Aldershot, 1952).
6. FSC, 14 January, 1825: No. 1, Minute, Sir Edward Paget, 15 December: also see J.W. Fortesque, *A History of the British Army*, Vol. 11 (1815-1838) (London, 1923) pp. 255-268.
7. *Ibid.*
8. Swinton to Nicol, 14 January: Brian Hodgson, Acting Resident Kathmandu, February 1825 in which he made a case for absorbing surplus Gorkhas in the Nepal Army into the Company's forces.
9. *Ibid.*, No. 22-23. Nicol to Swinton, 8 January.
10. K.L. Pradhan, "Brian Hodgson at the Kathmandu Residency", unpublished Ph.D. dissertation, North Eastern Hill University, 1986; Chapter I, for a fuller discussion of the subject.
11. FSC; 2 May, 1826, No. 14-15, 5th April, 1828, Neufville to Scott.
12. For details see J.B. Bhattacharjee, *Cachar under British Rule in North East India* (New Delhi, 1977) p. 52.
13. M.C. 14 October, 1830, No. 133.
14. H.K. Barpujari, *Problem of the Hill Tribes: North East Frontier*, Vol. I, (Gauhati, 1970) pp. 46 ff. DR Sylemlieh, *British Administration in the Meghalaya* (New Delhi, 1989) pp. 47 ff.
15. FPC: 23rd July, 1832, No. 9.
16. *Ibid.*, 1831.
17. *Ibid.*
18. FPC: 23rd July, 1832, No. 9, Minute by Governor-General Lord William Bentinck.
19. *Ibid.* This was the second battalion of the Kumaon Corps.
20. FPC: 27 August, 1832; No. 87; Report on Cachar; 15 October, 1832; No. 114; Report on Manipur.
21. Captain G.E. Westmacott, "Notes on the History of Assam", Ms 2217/3, Aberdeen University, Scotland, by kind permission of Professor Imdad Hussain.
22. The Shan Militia formed the nucleus of the Assam Rifles. For details see Imdad Hussain, "Shah Militia: Origins of the Para-Military System in Assam" in J.B. Bhattacharjee (Ed.) *Studies in the History of North East India* (Shillong, 1986).
23. FPC: 13 April, 1835; No. 59: Jenkins to Macnagthen, 27 March.

24. FPC: 19 February, 1835: Nos. 1-5; Minutes, Bentinck, 1 February.
25. *Ibid.* General orders by the Governor-General in Council, 98 of 1835. Also *Asiatic Journal and Monthly Register* etc., Vol. 29, 1839, Pt 2, 217.
26. Unlike his earlier proposal of separate Companies Jenkins now decided to confine recruitment to the Rabhas. The Kacharis, Jenkins found to be "a wilder race, duller and less tractable." FPC: 13 April, 1835: No. 59; Jenkins to Macnaghten, 26 February.
27. FDPC, 13 April, 1835, No. 59, Jenkins to Macnaughten in Political Department, 27 March 1835.
28. FPC: 24 May, 1843: No. 85, From Captain Mainwarring.
29. FPC: 5 August, 1843: No. 132; Fisher to Jenkins, 6 May.
30. FPC: 24 August, 1844; No. 51, General orders by the Governor-General in-Council No. 234 of 1844.
31. Each Company consisting of one Subadar, one Jemadar, four Havildars, five Naiks, one Bugler and eighty men.
32. BJP, 12 April, 1855. No. 160 and 791, F.D. Atkinson to Jenkins.
33. BJP, 12 April, 1855. No. 160 and 791, 27 March. Robert Campbell to Jenkins 13 February, 1855. The extra Recruit Department first came into operation when the 1st Assam Sebundy corps was redesignated as the Assam Light Infantry, and was subsequently abolished in July 1848.
34. F.D. Atkinson, Military Secretary to Jenkins, No. 21: 20 February, 1855.
35. FPC: 1 June *Ibid.,* 66-67.
36. BJP, 27 February, 1850: No. 36, Lister's Report, 2 February.
37. BJP, 14 August, 1850: No. 90.
38. BJP, 22 June, 1845: Nos. 158-59.
39. *Ibid.*
40. Sir Alexander Mackenzie, *History of the Relation of the Government with the Hill Tribe on the North East Frontier of Bengal* (Calcutta, 1884), pp. 116.
41. *Ibid.* Holroyd to Jenkins.
42. A.J.M. Mills, *Report on the Province of Assam* (Calcutta, 1854) *vide* Appendix No. Jenkins to Mills, 21 May, 1853.
43. *Ibid.* ASR letters issued to Government, Vol. 21, Series 11, Jenkins to Buckland, 20 August, 1856.
44. General orders by Commander-in-Chief, No. 523, 24.
45. H.K. Barpujari: Problem of the Hill Tribes: North-East Frontier (Gauhati, June 1976) 1843-72 Vol. II.
46. Diary of Sergeant Major George Carter, India Office Library and Records, by kind permission of Professor Imdad Hussain.

47. Hiralal Singh: *Problems and Policies of the British in India* (1963) Chapter III, General Hugh Rose thus hold Sir Charles Wood, 26 February, 1862, "I wish to have a different and rival spirit in different regiments, so that Sikhs might fire into Hindoo, Gorkha into either, without any scruple, in case of need."
48. K.M.L. Saxena: *The Military System of India 1850-1900* (New Delhi, 1974).
49. General orders by Commander-in-Chief, No. 400, (3 May) 1861.
50. Lieutenant F.G. Cardew: *Sketch of the Series of the Bengal Native Infantry* (New Delhi, 1971).
51. *Ibid.*
52. K.M.L. Saxena: *op cit.,* (New Delhi 1974), pp. 93-94.
53. M.P. November, 1862: No. 729, Norman to Adjutant General, 25 November. Also see K.M.L. Saxena *op cit.,* pp. 80-90.
54. Colonel H.L. Huxford: *History of the 8th Gorkha Rifles*, (Aldershot, 1952), p. 23.
55. H.K. Barpujari: *op. cit.* pp. 120-133.
56. BJP, July 1861: Nos. 252-253; Campbell to Hopkinson, 22 May, to Jenkins, 7 June.
57. Assam Secretariat, letters from Misc. Quarters, Series X, Vol. 24, 1860; BJP, June 1861, Nos. 387-88; Showers to Adjutant General.
58. Selection from the Records of the Government of Bengal, No. XXIX, Part I, Papers Relating to the Disturbances in the Cossyah and Jaintia Hills, Calcutta, 1863. Colonel Richardson thus wrote of his problem: "For a less extensive disturbance (in 1860) we had 500 or 600 at our immediate disposal, whereby opposition was at once put down. At present (against) 15,000 men capable of bearing arms, and everyone against us, I came with difficulty if at all, collect 200 men." To Assistant Adjutant General, Presidency, 29 January, 1861.
59. MP, December 1862, No. 525-27, Showers to Adjutant General, 10 September.
60. BJP, June 1863: No. 377.
61. MP, May 1865: No. 137: Haythorne to Norman, 29 April. Also see D.F. Rennie: *Bhotan and the Story of the Doar War,* (London 1866), p. 202.
62. *Ibid.* Norman to Haythorne, 18 May, Millitary Secretary to Secretary of State, No. 234, 1 June.
63. MP, July 1865, No. 145. From Bengal Government, 23 May Sir Cecil Beadon, Lieutenant Governor to Governor General-in-Council.
64. *Ibid.,* No. 146, Norman to Haythorne, 21 June.
65. *Ibid.,* No. 147, Norman to Haythorne, 15 July, also see Military Letter to Court No. 335, 15 August, 1865.
66. MP, February 1866, No. 278, Colonel Paton to Military Secretary, 23 December, 1865.

67. DGJ Ryan: *Historical Records of the 6th Gorkha Rifles, 1817-1919*, Vol. I, (Aldershot, 1925), pp. 23.
68. *Ibid.*
69. MP, September, 1868: Nos. 1-4, Hopkinson to Bengal, 13 March.
70. MP, December, 1867: Nos. 222-225.
71. H.L. Huxford: History of the 8th Gorkha Rifles, (Aldershot, 1952), p. 23.
72. H.L. Huxford: *op. cit.*, p. 24.
73. Foreign Political A February 1880: Nos. 264-274, Brigadier-General J.L. Nation to Quarter Master General, 16 September, 1879.
74. H.L. Huxford, *op. cit.*, p. 31.
75. For details, B.B. Mishra, *Administrative History of India* (London, 1970), p. 537; Sir Percival Griffiths. *To Guard My People' History of the Indian Police,* pp. 87ff. C.E. Buckland: *Bengal Under Lieutenant Governors*, (Calcutta, 1901) vol. 11, p. 231ff.
76. Imdad Hussain, "Shan Militia; Origin of the Para-Military System in Assam" in J.B. Bhattacharjee (ed.) *Studies in the History of North-East India* (Shillong, 1986).
77. B. Police P., October 1873: No. 33, Ac Lyall to Bengal, 30 September.
78. H Police B.P., March 1880; 27A-28; June 1880. p. 35-36.
79. H.P.P., March 1878: Nos. 33-37.
80. Alexander Mackenzie, *op. cit.* Appendix F, pp. 495-501. Note by the Chief Commissioner on the military requirements of Assam, 12 August, 1879.
81. *Ibid.* p. 504. Bernard to Chief Commissioner, 27 March, 1880. Bayley himself modified his military requirements after the Angami Naga uprising in 1879-80; Lyall to Government of India, 28 July, 1880.
82. *Ibid.*
83. Assam Rifles Manual. (Shillong, 1927), "Historical Records of the Assam Rifles", pp. VI ff.
84. Quoted in Alexander Mackenzie, *op. cit.*, p. 501.
85. Kanchanmoy Mojumdar: *Political Relations between India and Nepal 1877-1923* (New Delhi, 1973), p. 43, see also by the same author, *Anglo-Nepalese Relations in the 19th century* (Calcutta, 1973), chapter IX.
86. For Details, *Ibid.*
87. Byron Farwell, *The Gurkhas,* (London, 1984), p. 76.
88. *Assam Rifles Manual,* Preface.
89. For the Paujdeh Incident which was the climax of the Russian difficulty, see Rose Loise Greaves, *Persia and the Defence of India, 1884-1892.* (London, 1959).
90. Leo Rose, *Nepal Strategy for Survival* (USA, 1971), p. 141.
91. For Lord Roberts own views see his *Forty one Years in India* (Bently, 1897). Also G Macmun, *Martial Races in India* (Delhi, 1979).

92. M.P. 15, March, 1894, p. 207 (23 April, 1894).
93. Minute by Lord Roberts, 4 September, 1891, cited in Mojumdar *op. cit.,* p. 60.
94. The inferiority of physique was perhaps due to the causes referred to by Captain Vansittart, *viz.*, the restriction of recruiting operations and the exclusion of other districts which were quite capable of supplying good recruits if they were properly worked by selecting recruiters who were residents of these districts. A general statement regarding the inferiority of Gorkhas of Eastern Nepal cannot be accepted as a sufficiently weighty reasons for a re-consideration by Government orders.
95. Mojumdar *op. cit.*, p. 62, Bir Samsher was subsequently elevated to a GCSI.
96. *Assam Rifles Manualm, op. cit.,* p. ix.
97. *Ibid.*
98. FEBP, June 1909, Nos. 6-7, Notes, Report by CJ Stevenson Moore, Director of Criminal Intelligence.
99. *Military Handbook of General Information on India.* (Simla, 1908).
100. Assam Rifles Manual *op. cit.* p. xiii.
101. For details see among others H.K. Barpujari, *Problem of Hill Tribes North East Frontier*, Volume III (Gauhati, 1981), Chapter VIII.
PL Mehra, *McMohan Line and After*, (Madras, 1974) p. 171. ff.
D.P. Choudhury, *The North East Frontier of India 1865-1914* (Calcutta, 1979).
Alistair Lambs, two-volume study, *The McMohan Line*, is not readily available to Indian schollars.
102. H. Police A, April 1915, Nos. 73-92, Letter from the Chief Commissioner of Assam, 14 July, 1913.
103. H. Police A, April 1915, Nos. 73-92, Adjutant General's Branch.
104. Assam Judicial Police A Proceedings, March 1916, Nos. 8-22. (Inspection report recorded by GOC 8th (Lucknow) Division, 26th March, 1915).
105. H. Police A.P., November 1918, Nos. 95-96, J.E. Webster, Secretary Government of India, Home Department, 12 August, 1918.
106. Major General D.K. Palit, *Sentinels of the North East* (The Assam Rifles), (New Delhi, 1984) p. 59.
107. *Assam Rifles Manual*, Chapter VII, p. 51.

4

Punitive Expeditions in the Hills

After the annexation of Assam one of the major constraints faced by the British was "the task of pacifying and humanizing the primitive hill people"[1] inhabiting the surrounding hills of Assam. These hill tribes were always embroiled in internecine feuds among themselves, fighting clan with clan, family with family and indulging in kidnapping and murder of one another's men and live-stocks. It was also the habitual practice of most of the tribes to make trans-frontier forays into the foothills of Assam causing great amount of depredation and loss of lives and properties of the peaceful British subjects. The peace and tranquility of Assam borders had been constantly disturbed by this kind of aggression of the marauding tribes. The Nagas of Khonoma and Mozema villages were the most habitual offenders of breaking peace of the border lands inhabited by the non-tribals. They penetrated into the districts of Nowgong and Cachar, often to obtain slaves through the agency of Bengali traders, a class who, it was found, carried on a regular slave trade.[2] The possession of the heads of alien men, women and children and displaying them in the portals of their houses were the ethno-centric cult of these tribes particularly of the Nagas and they kept this tradition alive with utmost zeal and enthusiasm.

All the Government efforts to conciliate the tribes through peaceful and friendly means failed to dissuade the warring communities from their traditional barbaric incursion with slaughter, arson and rapine. At one point of time Lord Dalhousie found the Nagas as unbending as ever, he had no option but to withdraw altogether from the hills allowing the tribes to cut each others throats to their hearts content. In such situations the only choice left to the British was to assert British authority over the tribes and bring them under a system suited to the circumstances. This led the Government, eventually, to undertake drastic actions by way of punitive expeditions against the offenders.

After the treaty of Yandaboo, hardly a couple of years had elapsed when the first trouble occurred in the western Assam border with Doars on 22 October, 1828. The Dumpa Raja of Bhutan entered into the village Batakuchi in the north Kamrup district, seized several persons who were said to have been refugees from his jurisdiction and along with them the person who harboured them. The Government sent a police party to enquire into the matter but the Dumpa Raja made a treacherous attack on them and killed the party including the officer-in-charge and carried off a number of villagers into captivity. David Scott, Agent to the Governor General of India, for North Eastern Frontier, promptly sent a military force against Dumpa Raja and annexed the Doar region bordering Bhutan. David Scott posted therein a detachment who effected the release of the captives.

While the Bhutanese were causing a considerable anxieties and the Company was contemplating to take more drastic actions to quell them, the Khasis of Nongkhlaw became restive and rebellious under the leadership of U Tirot Sing, the Syiem of Nongkhlaw syiemship. They were protesting against the construction of a road through Nongkhlaw state to provide a link between Assam and Sylhet. This road was being constructed by David Scott, Agent of the Governor General of India with preliminary permission of U Tirot Sing, the Syiem of Nongkhlaw. On 4 April, 1829 more than four hundred Khasis burned down the convalescent bungalow at Nongkhlaw, killed several men including Captain Richard Bedingfield and set free the convicts engaged in construction of the road. Lieutenant Phillip Burlton escaped from the attack firing gallantly and keeping the enemies at bay but after fleeing down the hill about twenty miles forlorn, he was thoroughly exhausted and fell down whereupon the Khasis took him off and killed him. A punitive expedition was ordered to be undertaken immediately to quell the uprising. A military force consisting of the Sylhet Light Infantry, 23rd Bengal Infantry and a strong detachment of armed Civil Police, all under the command of Captain Lister entered Khasi Hills. With him also went Lieutenants Townshend, Vetch and Brodie.[3] The Khasi insurgents put up a strong resistance under the leadership of Tirot Sing and his follower Monbot supported by other syiems like Bormanik Syiem of Mylliem, Zubbar Sing, Syiem of Rambrai etc. David Scott thought that coercive measures such as burning of villages might induce the Khasis to submission "but motive of humanity, if not of policy forbid the adoption of such measures"[4]. The Khasis faced the British military expedition boldly fighting with their bows and arrows for which Governor General, William Bentinck referred this uprising as "the bow and arrow insurrection"[5]. However, the Khasis could not hold on for long against their superior armed enemies. Bormanik Syiem entered into an agreement with the Company on 15 January, 1830 in which he ceded a stretch of land to the south east of the Umiam river, relinquished his claim over Des Dumaria, agreed to become dependent on the Company and to pay a fine of Rs. 5000[6]. This led to break down of the unity and strength of the insurgency and by April 1830 almost entire Khasi Hills had been subdued including the whole of Mylliem, Rambrai, and Nongkhlaw together with the southern fringe of the hills in Mawmluh, Mawsmai and Byrong.[7] On 9 June, 1832 Jeet Roy, the Minister of Tirot Sing intimated Lieutenant Ingle the desire of his master to surrender on condition that his life would be spared. The latter consented and guaranteed the condition by taking oath after the custom of the Khasis. Accordingly, Tirot Sing accompanied with a party of thirty bowmen appeared before Henry Ingles and surrendered on 13 January, 1833. After a brief hearing at Gauhati on 26 January, 1832 Tirot Sing was sentenced to transportation of life to Tenasserim. He was subsequently, confined to house arrest in Dacca where he passed away on 17 July, 1835.[8]

The Nagas, one of the most formidable and troublesome hill tribes of the North East Frontier had been habitually raiding into the foothills of Assam around Nowgong and Cachar breaking the peace and order and often abducting plains people for slaves. Their incursions into Cachar was motivated by the "desire for plunder to obtain grain, cloths, conch-shells, slaves and scalp."[9]

The captured slaves were sold out to a class of Bengali traders who carried on slave business in the neighbouring districts.[10] "The strongest and the most turbulent of the Naga villages who were habitually engaged in such incursions were Mozema, Khonoma Jotsoma, Kohima and Kekrima, all of whom were well defended and contained each of them 700 to 800 houses."[11] In order to put a stop to this menace Mr. Grange conducted an expedition in January 1839 with 50 men of the Cacher Levy and a small detachment of the 1st ALI. The journey into the Naga Hills involved much climbing through forest-clad ranges over 500 feet in altitude. They reached some Naga villages on their way who were not aggressive and, thus there was no fighting or firing except a few shots against the fleeting offenders. Grange caught hold of a couple of headmen who took oath not to molest British village again. Finding no offenders or any case of slave capture Grange returned back to headquarters with his men *via* Dimapur.

After a year Mr. Grange undertook another expedition, with a stronger force this time, composed of detachments from the Cachar Levy, the Jorhat Militia and 50 men of the 1st ALI. The force marched *via* Raziphima up the Barail range 8000 feet height and proceeded towards Khonoma but the moment they arrived Typhini valley the party was greeted by series of stiff oppositions by the Nagas who set fire on the tall grass and rolled down rocks upon the advancing force. Reaching Chekwema (Yang) village the force found the village deserted and so they burnt it down. As the party advanced further towards Paplongmai the people of that village ambushed the force. "A fierce fight took place, continuing up to the village which was then destroyed including all grain and property that could be found."[12] The force also captured eleven prominent leaders of the Nagas, while the sepoys also suffered some casualties. Mr. Grange admitted those wounded sepoys at Dimapur hospital and went back to the hills with other men to continue the expedition. The force climbed up to two villages, viz. Piphima and Sephema who had earlier joined the Naga villages to attack the force. The Nagas of Piphima and Sephema resisted further advancement of the force with all their might. After a brief skirmish the Nagas gave way and fled into the jungle. The force destroyed both the villages.

In 1841, Captain Biggel undertook a peace mission in the Angami country and succeeded to some extent in pacifying the Nagas and awakening in them a confidence in the *bona fides* of the Government. Encouraged by such prospect the Angami leaders came down to Nowgong in 1842 and signed an agreement with I.T. Gordon, Principal Assistant, agreeing to pay tribute and to abstain from waging wars amongst themselves. But in January 1844 when Brown Wood, Sub-

Assistant, Golaghat, went up to collect tribute, the Mozoma and Khonoma clans flatly refused and defied the authority of the Government.[13]

In 1844, an outpost of the Cachar Levy situated at Hosang Hajoo in the North Cachar Hills was attacked by some recalcitrant Nagas killing a few Levies. After having established the fact that the attackers were people of Mozema village assisted by Asaloo village Mr. Woods was sent over the border with 50 men of the 1st ALI and 70 of the Cachar Levy to suppress them. The force reached both the Mozema and Asaloo villages and burnt down the Naga houses with the least opposition. After an army post was established at Samagutting "some kind of peace was maintained in that region and the Nagas began to submit themselves to the Government authorities. A thousand Angamis visited the fair at Nowgong to trade with the merchants in salt and cornelian beads .... and the utmost goodwill was manifested towards the authorities and the people of the plains."[14] But despite this, the Nagas thwarted every agreement with the Government and acted in the manner of utter defiance to the authorities. "Hardly a year passed when several women of Hassang Hajo were killed by the Bermah Nagas whose chief was in alliance with the Government."[15] In late November 1850 Captain Reid of the Artillery and Leutenant Bivar with an detachment and two three-pounder guns advanced on Mozema. Major Foquett and Captain Butler reached the village on 7th December and attacked the village. On the 10th, Butler reported that the mortar shell failed to hit the target because of dense fog and the narrow ridge of the mountain on which the enemy's position was situated. The two three-pounder guns were then advanced but the defence being very strongly constructed of stone and timber the guns were advanced within seventy yards. On reaching the defence, a deep and wide trench stopped all further progress. The force being exposed to showers of spears, musketry and stones obliged to retire to the spot where guns first opened fire and there bivouacked for the night. The next morning of the 11th, the friendly Nagas reported that the enemy had evacuated the fort and our troops immediately took possession of it. Thus in the long run Khonoma passed under the control of the British troops. Later on the hostiles were hunted out from their hideouts and a number of villages, viz. Sephema, Kegoma, Kekroma were destroyed.[16] The Nagas were punished and villages were destroyed but the unbending attitude of the Nagas and their indomitable courage and tenacity haunted the minds of the British with the hundred million dollar question—will it be justified to continue the punitive action against this turbulent tribe ? Butler, who was directly involved in the fight, wanted to leave the Nagas "entirely to themselves": Vincent, on the other hand, proposed permanent annexation of Angami county. The controversy was finally put a stop to, in 1853 by the Governor General, Dalhousie's decision as per the minute dated 21 February, which reads as follows:

> "Our future policy ought to be to confine ourselves to our own frontier, to protect it, as it could and ought to be protected, never to meddle in fights and feuds of those savages, to encourage trade with them so long as they were peaceful towards us, rigidly to exclude them all communications either to sell or to buy, on their becoming turbulent or troublesome."[17]

In the Lushai Hills (now Mizo Hills) which lies on the southern flank of Assam the Lushais (or Kukis as the old records call them) posed a serious problem. The Lushais and the Manipuris had been in constant war and enmity over the possession of land and other disputes. In April 1844, Lalchokla, a Mizo chief suddenly raided Kachubari, a Manipuri village south-east of Sylhet killing twenty persons and carrying off six into captivity. This was an aggression on a territory under the protection of the British. A party of Sylhet Light Infantry under Captain Blackwood advanced into the Lushai Hills and took possession of Lalchokla's village. The Lushai Chief surrendered to the force on condition that his life would be spared and that he would not be put to jail. But after a brief trial he was convicted of murder and sentenced to transportation for life. This act of treachery on the part of British was never forgotten nor forgiven by the Lushais. They were waiting for an opportune time to take a befitting revenge. In November 1849 the Lushais under the leadership of Vonpilal raided a Manipuri village named Rupchera, ten miles from Silchar where twenty-nine persons were killed and forty-two carried off. To punish the offenders Government of Bengal directed Colonel Lister, Commandant SLI to proceed immediately to deal against the aggressors. Accordingly, in early January 1850, Col. Lister proceeded with 1000 of SLI and 150 armed Civil Police and on reaching the place launched a sudden attack on Mora, a large Lushai village with 800 houses, killed six people, destroyed the village and burned the granaries, taking advantage of the absence of the Lushai chief and his fighting men. Thereafter, Col. Lister made a hasty retreat lest he would be caught and cut off in the jungles.

It was decided that the winter reconnaissance which was usually carried out in order to train officers as well as to collect information should be conducted in the Chittagong Hill Tracts. Accordingly in January 1888 two such reconnaissance parties were dispatched from Calcutta to Rangamati from where the parties were to start the work. As no hostility on the part of the Lushais was anticipated, so only very small escorts of 10 Frontier Police were allotted to each party. Both the parties carried out the reconnaissance work smoothly for about a couple of weeks without any obstruction. Mr. Stewart engaged three of the Frontier Police to look after his elephant at the base camp and proceeded up the hill about a day's march with the rest of his party to work. On the 2nd February, 1888 night after the day's hard work the party had just gone to sleep putting one escort on sentry duty, Stewart was standing partially dressed outside the little hut and his servant handing a cup of tea; suddenly there was a rush of shouting savages with muskets, spears and daggers who attacked them unprepared. Everything was at once a confusion, the sentry was shot dead, two corporals were stabbed to death. As the Police Havildar was trying to reach his rifle he was shot dead, while other two police escorts managed to get at their rifles and returned the fire. Stewart retired up the hill-side firing from his revolver but was shot at the edge of a ravine where he fell dead. As soon as the news reached Rangamati, Mr. Murray, the Deputy Superintendent of Police with a escort proceeded to the spot and buried the headless bodies, (heads being carried off and all weapons, ammunitions and personal belongings having been taken away).

Hardly had the arrangements for sending an expedition to punish the wrong doers of this massacre been given effect to when another raid was committed by a group of Lushais led by three Chiefs, viz. Nikama, Kairuma and Lungliama who made a lightening attack on the border village, about four miles from Demagiri killing the

Chieftainess with more than twenty of her people and carrying off fifteen persons. A military action against the offenders was ordered under command of Brigadier General Tregear which comprised 1250 of all ranks. The government policy of punitive expedition was, however, drastically changed from killing and burning of villages to (1) making of road to connect the villages, (2) establishing a permanent post at some suitable place, and then (3) punishing the wrong doers.

On 3rd April, 1853 one of the most fateful and heinous crime was committed by the Mozoma Nagas against the Cachari Chief. On the ground of retaliation for the previous outrage the Mozoma Nagas burnt the Cachari village Semkhar, adjacent to British territory, killed 80 men and carried off 115 captives.[18] Nakulram, son of Tularam rushed against the Nagas with 300 men who was trapped by Nagas and hacked to death while many others who accompanied him also met the same fate. On receipt of this atrocious massacre, Jenkins directed the Principal Assistant, Nowgong to send a detachment immediately to prevent the aggressive Nagas from indulging in such atrocities. However, Bivar informed the Agent that nothing sort of military action would effectively prevent the recurrence of Naga atrocity as long as the Cacharis themselves remain vulnerable to such aggression.[19] In a similar strain, Jenkins communicated through his letter on June 5, 1854 to Frederick Halliday, the Lieutenant Governor of Bengal that the only prospect to putting an end to the incursions of the Nagas was the annexation of their country.[20] This suggestion of Jenkins, however, did not impress the Lieutenant Governor who felt that the Agent had made no serious attempt to explain to the Nagas the policy of the government. Accordingly on March 2, 1855 Frederick Halliday advised Jenkins to make it clear to the Nagas that the government had –

> "no wish to interfere in the smallest degree with their independence and are at all times willing, so long as they conduct themselves in a peaceful and friendly manner, to receive them in our territories in a similar spirit when they desire to resort there for trade and other purposes."[21]

This principle of non-interference with the internal feuds of the tribals was more or less adhered to in respect of the Garos also with whom there had been a few skirmishes and any such coercive measures had proved ineffective. The Garos were the first of the hill tribes the British came into contact with, when in 1765 the districts of Dacca, Mymensing and Rongpur were taken over from the Mahommedan Diwani of Bengal. The Garos, not being a very outrageous race like the Nagas and Lushais, were not involved in major punitive expedition in the past. According to the account of them as given by Col. L.W. Shakespear "only three small raids had to be punished with, in one case, the burning of a village, but there was no active opposition."[22] The last expedition undertaken against the Garos was in 1874 by a detachment of 200 sepoys and 500 armed Civil Police under Captain Williamson, Davis and Mr. Daly. After they were punished by this expedition the Garos turned completely submissive and peaceful and co operated with government in everything. In 1879 the Headquarters of civil administration was moved from Goalpara to Dhubri and Garo Hills was controlled from the Tura administrative unit.

On the northern bank of the river Brahmaputra, proceeding towards the east of Bhutan there lived a variety of hill tribes occupying contiguous areas along its whole length with distinct cultures, dialects and manners. They are known, serially, as the Akas, Daflas, Miris, Abors, Mishmis, Khamtis and the Singphos. These hill tribes were the source of constant trouble and breach of peace by their frequent forays in the neighbouring plains districts under British government. During 1854-57 no less than six outrages were committed in which over twenty six persons were killed, four wounded and fifteen carried off into captivity. In 1830 one Thagi Raja, the chief of the Akas caused considerable trouble along the border of Darrang district through an attack on the Charduar stocked near Balipara.

In 1854 a band of Mishmis murdered two French missionaries who happened to enter their territory. To punish the offending tribe a detachment of ALI under Lieutenant Eden rushed to the hills. After eight days of arduous march, the party reached the offender village, captured the murderer Kai-ee-sha and burnt down the village. The accused murderer Kai-ee-sha was hanged to death after a brief trial. In 1899 the Bebejia clan of Mishmi raided a village sixteen miles from Sadiya, killing several people and carrying off many others for slaves. A punitive expedition was ordered under the command of

Colonel Molesworth with 44 Gorkha Rifles. The party left Sadiya in November 1899 and arrived at Hunli and Kaladoi villages. There was no opposition from the offender villages. The elders of the two villages surrendered, paid fine and returned back the captives. The expedition party returned back to Sadiya on 8 February, 1900. In 1871 the Daflas suddenly raided a village inside British territory carrying off 35 persons and killing others. To punish the offenders a force of 1000 rifles of the 1st and 2nd ALI and a strong detachment of Dibrugarh Frontier Police was sent under Colonel Stafford. The Daflas, being not warlike people, made no opposition, returned the captives and paid the imposed fine.

The Chulikatta Mishmis also started trouble by raiding into the Sadiya area, for which it became expedient to send a punitive expedition. Accordingly, a detachment of 125 rifles of the 2nd Assam Rifles under Captain R.P. Abigail and Lieutenant J. Murray Grant was dispatched along with O'Callagham, Political Officer. Before the force reached the destination the Mishmi held a stockaded position to oppose the advancing party. There was a fight between the two parties in which the Mishmis lost a considerable number of men including the leader of the clan. The village was destroyed, fines imposed on them and two posts were left for a few months to keep control of that part of the country. In recognition of the excellent work rendered during this period by Jamadar Surbir Ale, 2nd Assam Rifles, this officer was rewarded by presentation of the coveted King's Police Medal. Subadar Major Jongbir Lama's long and good services were also recognized by the title of "Sirdar Bahadur" being bestowed on him.[23]

But the most turbulent amongst the tribals of this region were the Abors who inhabited among the river basins of Dihang, Dibong and Lohit and carried on the occupation of gold washing in these rivers. A dispute arose in 1848 between the Abors and the Miris and Cacharis over the sharing of the gold washing areas among them which culminated in killing and carrying off of a number of Miris and Cacharis by the Abors. An expedition with a strong detachment of 2nd ALI was dispatched from Sadiya which reached their village and inflicted a deterrent punishment on the offenders, burnt their village and imposed heavy fine. The Abors were, however, unbending and ever aggressive for which frequent punitive actions had to be carried out. In 1858 the Abors raided a village of Beheas (a small community) and killed twenty-one persons and wounded six for a minor reason. A strong detachment of the ALI under the command of Captain W.H. Lowther proceeded to the village of occurance while getting the news in advance, the whole Meyong clan of Abor gathered together and waited for the fight well-prepared. Fearing that the security of the British subjects would be endangered, the Abors were given a free hand. The government decided to dispatch another expedition in a manner as would ensure complete success. Accordingly, in early 1859 another expedition was organised with elaborate scale of force under Colonel Hannay, Commandant of ALI aided by Major Reid of the Local Artillery. The force reached the village and stormed the hideouts of the enemy and easily captured their stronghold. The force advanced further and destroyed another two villages. But the Meyongs remained unbending and aggressive as ever.

Use of Gun Powder and Muskets

During these expeditions it was found that many of the tribes had learnt to use muskets with gun powder. More prominent of them were the Lushais, Nagas and the Kukis. The Lushais were better armed than most other north eastern tribes, as they possessed a considerable number of old percussion or flint-lock muskets, many of which were English make, tower marked and some were stamped with makers name 'Alton', while others had French marks. It is learnt that they had begun to learn making rough but still fairly useful gun powder and the use of firearms from the Burmese since about a decade past from whom they acquired gun powder. A regular trading in these arms and ammunitions seems to have started in the early seventies from Burma, Bengal and Cachar and by that time Lushais, Kukis and Nagas were in possession of considerable number of weapons. They loved and held these firearms as trophies and decorated the butts and stocks with paint and varnish of various colours and often embellish their powder flasks, made of mithun horn, with silver or ivory inlaids. In the beginning, gun powder was made by the tribes from sulphur which they obtained from Burma as it was not available in the hills. After 1885 when export of sulphur was stopped by government they started preparing it by soaking and boiling the 'aunglauk' bean which contained much sulphur. It is presumed that these hill tribes must have learnt the art of processing sulphur from the Ahoms who had the knowledge of doing this ever since 17th century, when they used cannons with gun powder against the Mohammedans in 1665, Mirjumla's invasion of Assam.

Synteng Rebellion

Reverting back to our discussion about punitive expedition in the hills, we turn now towards the southern hill tribes like the Syntengs or Jaintias and the Manipuris. The Synteng rebellion took place in 1860 in opposition against the house tax imposed on the people of Jaintia Hills. Ever since the annexation of Jaintia Hills in 1835, the people of Jaintia were not imposed any tax although each village, as a token allegiance, had to contribute a he-goat to the government annually. This was considered objectionable by AJM Mills who had been deputed to this district in 1854 to enquire into the judicial anomalies. He opined – "In the neighbouring hill tracts a house tax was paid and we are acting unwisely and inequitably in exempting Jayantias." In compliance with this report of AJM Mills a house tax was introduced in 1860. This act of the government was vehemently opposed by the Syntengs. The Tehsildar appointed by government for collection of house tax was forcibly expelled followed by a rebellion. The timely arrival of a force under Colonel Richardson from Cherra brought the situation under temporary control. The resentment of the people was spreading across the hills when imposition of income tax in early next year put a spark to the fire. On 17 January, 1862 the Syntengs numbering about six hundred made a surprise attack on the military guard at Jowai, burnt down the Christian settlement and thereafter retired and stockaded their village in the neighbourhood.[24] The principal scenes of action were in the area round Jowai, thirty-two miles east of Shillong which was besieged by the rebels for nearly three weeks. A strong force consisting of 21st and 28th Punjab Infantry, 33rd Native Infantry, 2nd ALI, SLI, the Kamrup Regiment was rushed to suppress the rebellion under the command of Colonel Dunsford which succeeded in dispersing the rebels with much difficulty and a number of casualties.[25] The villages of Jowai,

Amwai and Nungteng were occupied, stockades were demolished and granaries destroyed. Although the rebels had been dispersed and situation brought under control, the hard-core remained stubborn under the leadership of U Kiang Nongbah. The insurgency, in the mean time, spread throughout the district. The suppressive policies followed by Government, introduction of Judicial stamp and levy of taxation on fisheries which was hitherto free from assessment etc. led to scare the hill men that the English were determined "to stay and fleece them". In the same year the right to cut timber in certain areas was sold out to the highest bidder prohibiting the people to use timber, fuel and thatch. The Syntengs were greatly offended when the Deputy Commissioner confiscated their swords and shields and burnt them as a measure of disarming the rebels. Thus the rebellion, although began against the house tax, it took the form of freedom movement with the object of driving away the British (*phareng*) from the country. The deposed Raja of Jaintia, the Dolois and Sardars also took initiative in whipping up public opinion against the British. "Brisk preparations were made for the war of liberation by collecting arms, erecting stockades, storing up grains and sending emissaries for aid even to Burma."[26] With a view to stem the grave situation the government issued proclamation granting amnesty to all those who would lay down arms with exception of the ring leaders and those guilty of gross acts of aggression. A reward of rupees one thousand was offered to one who assist in capture of U Kiang Nongbah. The strong measures taken by the government broke down the morale of the insurgents. The Sirdars of Shampung, Galong and Munsow tendered their submission. The villagers gradually returned back to their homes and resumed normal occupations. But the main leaders headed by U Kiang Nongbah continued to defy the government by their determined acts of aggression. In a dorbar attended by hundreds of insurgents, U Kiang Nongbah announced their firm determination that there would be no compromise with the British unless the government withdraw all taxations, their ex-Raja was reinstated again and all the military force were withdrawn from the hills. On the night of 7th November,1862 the rebels attacked the village Terraghat killing a sepoy and two individuals. The government had no other option but to alter its policy for use of force. On 27th November, 1862 a detachment of 28 Native Infantry under the command of Lieutenant

Sadller and led by U Lung, a resident of Nartiang, succeeded in capturing U Kiang Nongbah at Umpara, a village 25 miles from Nartiang. It is said that U Kiang Nongbah was captured by an act of treachery hatched by his own men for the greed of reward declared by Government. A military trial was held where U Kiang Nongbah was found guilty of rebellion and was publicly hanged on 30 December, 1862. Among the other insurgent leaders, U Sawar, the Doloi of Sutnga, was shot dead in the encounter with the troops, U Chey Rangbah was killed, U Mon, the Doloi of Rymbai was murdered by his followers near Nartiang, U Bang, the Doloi of Ralliang surrendered and U Bukher, the Pator tendered his submission on condition of his life to be spared. Thus the Synteng rebellion was fully suppressed.

Manipur Tragedy

In Manipur, after the death of the Maharaja in 1886 he was succeeded by his son Sura Chandra but there was a dispute about his being the king. A rival claimant tried to seize the throne but the attempt was foiled by timely help of the Military Police from Cachar. However, in 1890 Sura Chandra was driven away from the throne by one Juvaraj with the help of Senapati Tikendrajit, Commander-in-Chief of the Manipur Royal Army. The deposed Raja, Sura Chandra once again sought for the intervention of the Government.

In March 1891, Mr. Quinton, Chief Commissioner of Assam left Shillong for Manipur to personally enquire into and settle up the dispute. From Golaghat he took his escort of 400 men of the 44th and the 42nd Gorkha Rifles under Colonel Skene. On being told that there was no likelihood of any offensive trouble in Manipur, the Chief Commissioner was accompanied by a minimum number of young soldiers, armed with Snider rifles, 40 rounds per man and took no reserve ammunition. So little was the threat perception that even the two mountain guns in possession of each of the Assam Gorkha Regiments were not taken along. The British officer with the column were Colonel Skene, Major T. Boileau, Captain Butcher, Chatterton, Gurdon, Lieutenants Brackenbury and Simpson, Mr. Cossins and Captain Woods. Reaching Imphal the Senapati and his associates, the main trouble makers, were asked to appear before the Durbar at the Residency. On his refusal to comply with the summons for three successive days, troops were sent into the palace enclosure to effect his arrest but they were fiercely attacked by the Manipuri personnel severely wounding Lieutenant Brackenbury. In the evening a proposal of armistice was received from the Senapati with an invitation to the Chief Commissioner accompanied by four officers for a talk inside the palace which was agreed to, in good faith, by the Chief Commissioner. Accordingly Mr. Quinton, Chief Commissioner together with Colonel Skene, Messrs. Grimwood, Cossins and Lieutenant Simpson entered the palace at 10.30 p.m. without carrying any arms on the assurance of safe and good conduct by the Senapati. But it turned out to be a ghastly treachery, none of them came out again—the officers were fatally wounded by spear-thrust and killed while the Chief Commissioner was beheaded by the public executioners in front of two stone dragons. Col. L.W. Shakespear ruefully questions as to "why the Chief Commissioner and party walked blindly into the trap, although it was stipulated that they should come unarmed and even at the gate the young orderly bugler with Colonel Skene was turned back by the Manipuri officer with the words, 'we don't want children here' which all might have given a fair hint as to likely treachery."[27]

With a view to exact adequate retribution against the outrage, three columns marched to Manipur from Kohima, Silchar and Tammo (Burma) of which the former two columns reached Imphal without any opposition while the last one experienced some fighting at Palel and again near Thobal. On arrival at Imphal the small Manipuri force was easily overpowered and disarmed, the palace was seized and the Senapati, Tikendrajit Singh was arrested together with Subadar Niranjan Singh and a few other associates suspected to be involved in the murder. They were tried and on 8 June, 1891 Tikendrajit Singh and Niranjan Singh were publicly hanged.

The punitive expeditions mentioned in the above paragraphs were among the major ones while there were other small punitive tours across the hill areas of North Eastern Frontier undertaken during and after 1900 which could not be mentioned here due to space constraint. The hostile character of the tribes, however, was found to have been gradually calming down as time passed and there were less number of raids by the Nagas and other tribes into the British territories. Roads and bridle paths were constructed and connectivity with interior villages was improved. Police outposts were established in the areas of more vulnerability. The work of civilizing the hill tribes began in right earnest. Schools and hospitals were established and the parents were encouraged to send their children to the schools. The tribes were taught to use modern medicine instead of believing on the quacks and the sick persons were encouraged to go to hospitals. The Christian missionaries began the task of proselytizing the tribes into Christianity especially in the hill aıeas. They introduced Roman script and wrote school reader books in tribal languages for children in the schools. The civilizing influence of the missionaries spread far and wide in the interiors. Thus the people in the hills gradually adapted themselves to the new situation and became less aggressive towards the British subjects. The tribes who had been accustomed in raiding and looting the foothill markets commenced to trade with the plains.

NOTES

1. Col L.W. Shakespear, *The History of Assam Rifles*, p. vii.
2. *Ibid.*, p. iii.
3. *Ibid.*, 12.
4. F.P.C., 31 December, 1830, No. 22.
5. C.H. Phillips, *The Correspondence of Lord William Bentinck*, Vol. I.
6. C.U. Atchinson, *op. cit.*, Vol. XII, 1931, p. 131-132.
7. N.K. Barooah, *op. cit.*, p. 207.
8. D.R. Syiemlieh, "New Light on Tirot Sing: His last days and demise," in *The North-Eastern Hill University Journal of Social Science and Humanities*, Vol. V, No. 4, October 1987, p. 27-30.
9. *Ibid.*
10. *Ibid.*, p. 16.
11. *Ibid.*
12. W.L. Shakespear, *History of Assam Rifles*, p. 19.
13. H.K. Borpujari, *Problems of the Hill Tribes: North East Frontier*, 1843-1872, p. 20.
14. J. Butler, *Travels and Adventures in Assam*, p. 173.
15. H.K. Borpujari, *op. cit.*, p. 28.
16. J. Butler, *op. cit.*, p. 198-99.
17. Political Letter to the Court, 21 April, 1853, No. 29.
18. BJP, 12 June, 1854, Nos. 174-75; Bivar to Jenkins, 4 May, 1853.

19. *Ibid.*, No. 182; Bivar to Jenkins, 1st July, 1853.
20. BJP, Jenkins, 5 June, 1854, 14 June, 1855, Nos. 186.
21. BJP, 8 March, No. 163, Grey to Jenkins, 2 March.
22. Col. L.W., Shakespear, *History of Assam Rifles*, p. 31.
23. Shakespear, p. 140.
24. Selection of Records, Government of Bengal, xvii, Rawlatt to the Secretary, Government of Bengal, 9 April.
25. Col. L.W. Shakespear, *The History of Assam Rifles*, p. 49.
26. H.K. Borpujari, *Problems of the Hill Tribes of North East, 1843-1872*, p. 81-82.
27. Shakespear, *op. cit.* p. 178.

5

Consolidation of British Rule

The British annexation of Brahmaputra Valley in 1826 was quickly followed by the process of consolidation of British rule in the whole of North East Frontier. David Scott, the Agent to the Governor General for Assam was a shrewd administrator who had a greater influence upon the Company's military affairs than any contemporary military officer had. He harboured in his heart the desire for extending British imperialism for which he urgently felt the need to strengthen Company's military power. In order to consolidate British rule in the newly appropriated North East Frontier he persuaded the Government of India to raise the Sylhet Light Infantry as early as 1924. For fulfilment of his imperial design, he drew up a plan to link up Assam with Sylhet, which was already a British territory, by constructing a road across Khasi Hills. With a preliminary agreement of U Tirot Sing, the Syiem of Nongkhlaw, construction of the road started from Bardwar which fell under the Syiemship of Nongkhlaw. However, Tirot Sing alone had no authority to confer the right to the usage of the land and the matter was to be considered and a consensus of the Syiem in Council was to be obtained in the Dorbar which later on was refused by the Dorbar sensing that the British would take their land. This led to Anglo-Khasi war in 1829 in which many other Syiems of Khasi hills joined hands with Tirot Sing. The war lasted for four years and in the long run, the Syiems surrendered one after another to the military might of the Company. Tirot Sing was captured and deported to Dacca in 1833.

Integration of Khasi Hills

After the conclusion of the Anglo-Khasi war in 1832 the British started consolidating their rule over the Khasi states through diplomacy and show of military power. Many of the Khasi chiefs had already tendered their allegiance to the Company for their protection from outsider through a series of treaties ever since 1829 up to 1856; among them were –Syiem Manik of Khyrim, Dewan Singh of Cherra, Sunder Singh of Langrin, Dur Singh of Nongspung and Mit Singh of Nongstoin. Other states of the Syiems and Sirdars were brought under the British rule through issue of Sunnads. The Political Agent to the Governor General was an overall charge of administration who uptil 1853 combined military and civil functions. After 1853 the civil department was separated from military and a Principal Assistant Commissioner was instituted in place of Political Agent. He was stationed at Cherrapunjee, the headquarters, from where he conducted the administration.

For smooth administration of Khasi Hills each Khasi state was categorized into semi-independent and dependent state. Five states, viz. Cherra, Khyrim, Nongstoin, Langrin and Nongspung were referred to as semi-independent states as they had never been actually coerced by British force.[1] The remaining twenty states were categorized as dependent states which were restored to their chiefs following the Anglo-Khasi war.[2] The semi-independent states enjoyed a little wider authority in exercise of criminal and civil powers than the dependent states. The heads of the semi-independent states were permitted to exercise with the aid of their Dorbars and the elders, sole criminal and civil jurisdiction in their respective states and over their own subjects as they did in their traditional system. The dependent chiefs were allowed to try minor civil and criminal cases in which the parties were their own people with the exception of the heinous cases of murder, homicide, dacoity with murder in which the maximum punishment is death. These cases were to be transferred to the Deputy Commissioner for trial. In cases where one of the parties are British subjects both the categories of states would have to refer the case to the district authorities for trial.

The British paramountcy was further extended in respect of appointment and discharge of the heads of the Khasi states and their functions. The Syiem was subject to the control and order of the Deputy Commissioner; and he is liable to be removed, suspended or appointed by the Deputy Commissioner. He should implicitly obey all lawful orders as would be issued by the Deputy Commissioner or any other government official acting on behalf of the Deputy Commissioner. The Syiem would also furnish adequate information on the condition of his subjects when so required by government and that the Syiem should reside in his state and not elsewhere.[3]

In 1864 the District Headquarters was shifted from Cherra to Shillong, which was situated in the heart of Mylliem Syiemship. Gradually Shillong grew up as civil and military Headquarters. In 1874 Shillong became the capital of Assam. The population and area of Shillong having increased, it was declared municipal area under Municipal Act (Assam Act of 1923) which included Mawkhar, Laban, Mawprem, Jhalupara and Malki villages.

In 1866 the 44th (Sylhet) regiment of Bengal Native (Light) Infantry moved into Shillong Headquarters from Cherrapunjee which comprised a good number of Gorkha soldiers. This 44th Light Infantry was subsequently designated as the 8th Gurkha Rifles. The Gorkha settlement in Shillong starts from this date while in 1891 a plot of land measuring approximately half a mile by one-fourth a mile was obtained on lease from the Syiem of Mylliem for the establishment of Regimental village for the Gorkha soldiers and civilians (*vide* Appendix III). The present Nepali populated area of Shillong known as Mawprem was the Gorkha regimental village.

With a view to spreading education in Khasi and Jaintia Hills the British inducted the Welsh Calvinistic Methodist Mission who were located at Sylhet. The Mission came to Cherrapunjee in 1842 and started their works of imparting education together with proselytizing the Khasis into Christianity. The Khasis and Jaintias had no script of themselves and, therefore, Rev. Thomas Jones introduced Roman script with some alterations suitable for the sound of Khasi language. Their Welsh nationality led them to use the vowel 'Y' for the obscure sound represented elsewhere in India by a short u as 'a' and for the consonantal 'y' to substitute the vowel 'I'. Primer books for the study of the language were printed at Calcutta in 1846 and 1852 and in 1855 appeared the excellent "Introduction to the Khasi language, comprising a grammar and a Khasi-English vocabulary." An exhaustive grammar, by H. Roberts, was published in 1891. Thus the Khasi and Jaintia people gradually became aware of the need of education and started sending their children to school and they themselves accepted Christianity.

Annexation of Jaintia Hills

The British annexation of Jaintia Hills may be ascribed to two reasons—firstly, the Raja of Jaintia had encroached on the southern border of the Nowgong district and the Raja had been evading compliance to the repeated request of the British government to remove the encroachment. Secondly, in 1832 Chatur Singh, the Raja of Gobha, one of the petty Chieftains dependent on Jaintia, acting on the order of his suzerain, kidnapped four British subjects, three of whom were sacrificed at the shrine of Goddess Kali. The fourth escaped and gave information to the government. The Raja of Jaintia was asked to hand over the culprits to the government to deal with according to law but the Jaintia king did not pay heed to the request for long two years during which time the Raja Ram Singh died and his nephew, Rajendra Singh succeeded. The government, therefore, decided to confiscate the plains portion of the Jaintia kingdom leaving the Raja to rule over the hills. Accordingly on 15 March, 1835 Captain Lister with two companies of Sylhet Light Infantry took formal possession of Jaintiapur and issued a proclamation announcing the annexation of Jaintia pargana to British territory. This was quickly followed by annexation of Gobha, in the Nowgong district to the British India. The Raja Rajendra Singh was left with only the hill areas of his kingdom which did not yield revenue enough to cover even the cost of administration. In sheer disappointment he declined to retain possession of the hills which, consequently, passed into the hands of the British. Thus, the whole of Jaintia kingdom was annexed to the British territory on flimsy ground of criminal offence committed by some miscreants. An Assistant to the Political officer was stationed at Jowai who looked after the administration of Jaintia Hills while the hill portion continued to be controlled by the Dolois and Sirdars. They were allowed to try all civil suits without limit and criminal cases not of heinous character in the nineteen *elakas* of the hills. Of these *elakas* fifteen were under a Doloi each, and thirteen Sirdars were in-charge of the remaining four divisions. Later on in 1841 the government fixed limitation on the judiciary powers of the Dolois and Sirdars. Their jurisdiction in civil suits was limited to the value of rupees fifty and in criminal cases the Dolois and Sirdars were prohibited trial of criminal cases in which their relatives and dependents were involved.

Anglo-Jaintia War

Rajendra Singh, the ex-Raja of Jaintia, had not yet forgotten the British annexation of his kingdom in March 1835 and the series of humiliations meted out to him by the East India Company. The royal families were greatly mortified with the loss of their ancestral property and the exclusion of their members from their old possessions or the profit whatever from this disposal.[4] The Dolois and Sirdars too were frustrated at the curtailment of their administrative and judiciary powers, and the people at large had turned hostile to the arrogance of the British officers and the presence of police around their hitherto peaceful country. The political atmosphere of Jaintia Hills was simmering with discontentment and hatred and was at the verge of explosion into a revolution. The immediate cause that hastened the revolution was the imposition of the house tax which was alien to the culture of the people of Khasi and Jaintia Hills. This led to the sudden break out of rebellion which was joined by both the Khasi and the Jaintia people.[5] On 28 March, 1860 a mob consisting of more than 200 people attacked the Police Station at Koina Ghat and plundered everything including arms and ammunitions. On 30 March the Police Station at Jaintiapur was looted.[6] A detachment of the Sylhet Light Infantry was immediately dispatched to Jaintiapur to quell the movement. In April further reinforcement of troops was brought from Dacca consisting of 260 strong. The movement gradually spread throughout the length and breadth of the country and took a turn towards the object of securing independence and restoration of the lost Jaintia kingdom. The Raja Rajendra and his heirs were deported to Dacca suspecting that the rebellion was instigated by them. The battle flared up under the able leadership of U Kiang Nongbah who was joined by many Dolois like—Giri Dolois of Shangpung, Myllon Doloi of Mynso, Bang Doloi of Nartiang, Suwar Doloi of Sutnga and the Dolois of Nongkhlieh and Rymbai. The Jaintia warriors used archery, indigenous matchlocks, swords and shields and resorted to guerrilla fighting. The British soldiers could not trace the direction from where the arrows came and were confounded[7]. Unable to capture the leader of the movement the Government announced handsome reward for the capture or giving information about U Kiang Nongbah. The reward provided immediate motivation to trap the hero of the uprising. According to local tradition it is said that U Kiang Nongbah was captured through treachery at Mynso in the winter of 1862 and was handed over to the British authority. A brief trial was held by the military Tribunal which found U Kiang Nongbah guilty of waging war against the government and was hanged to death. With his death the Jaintia rebellion came to a close.

Integration of Garo Hills

Integration of Garo Hills was comparatively easier as there was not much of resistance. The major problem faced by the British in Garo Hills was, however, stopping the menace of Garo raids on the foot-hills of British control. The Garos were confirmed head-hunters and a terror to the people of the plains. They rendered the border areas wholly insecure by their frequent raids for plunder and for procuring human skulls which they needed for funeral ceremonies.[8] The Zamindars demanded greater control of the Garos to save the life and property of the people. Accordingly Zamindars were allowed to maintain armed force for the purpose of collecting tribute from the tributary Garos falling within the estates of Karaibari, Mechpara and Kalumalupara. The exaction of the Zamindars often provoked these hill men to enter into the village and make forcible demands of grains, livestock and other necessaries. For many years the government followed a policy of non-interference but it did not succeed in establishing peace and order in Garo Hills as the Garos remained most irregular in payment of revenue.

The policy of non-interference having failed in 1869 the government formed a new district in Garo Hills with Tura as its headquarters but its general administration was still carried out from Goalpara. In 1871 Major Gordon Austen and Captain Williamson with an armed police escort were the first to traverse Garo hills for survey purpose.[9] Many of the Garo villages tendered their allegiance to the British without resistance but some remote villages were still stubborn. Two years later the Garos of Pharangiri village broke out in rebellion and attacked the police post causing minor casualties. In retaliatory expedition village was destroyed by Captain La Touche with forty armed constables. By 1874 the Garos were completely subjugated and the entire Garo Hills was integrated into British territory.

In 1879 the Headquarters of civil administration was moved from Dhubri to Tura and placed under Captain Williamson as Deputy Commissioner with a battalion of the Frontier Police of 300 men located at Tura. Gradually law and order were established in the whole of Garo Hills. For the dispensation of law and justice Laskars were appointed for collection of revenue and trial of cases of minor offences. They were given magisterial powers of the third class and entrusted to try small offences and disputes. Cases involving heinous crimes like murder, homicide, robbery etc. were to be transferred to the Deputy Commissioner for dealing with as per established law. Above the Laskars was placed a Sarbarkar who was responsible for the supervision of the Garo chiefs.[10]

Annexation of Naga Hills

The turbulent Nagas were the most unbending and refractory of all the hill tribes and initially it was no part of the British policy to annex Naga Hills into the British territory. We have seen in the preceding chapter how the Nagas thwarted every agreement and good gesture of the government and acted in a manner of utter defiance to the authorities. Butler who was directly involved in the punitive action against the Nagas wanted to leave them entirely to themselves. Nevertheless, for the interest of peace and order in the entire hill areas and for the purpose of civilizing the primitive hill tribes the government continued its policy of bringing them in the fold of British administration. With this end in view in 1866 it was resolved to take possession of the Angami country and reclaim its inhabitants from savagery. This tract and the watershed of Doyang were accordingly formed into a district with its Headquarters at Samaguting, but in 1878 Samaguting was abandoned in favour of Kohima which was made the District Headquarters. This was followed by the annexation of the country of Lhota Naga in 1875 and a British officer was posted there. In 1876 Okha was taken over by the British force and it was made the Sub-Divisional Headquarters. The last battle was fought by the Nagas registering their protest against British occupation of their country at village Khonoma on 22 December, 1879 in which many Nagas were killed. The Nagas surrendered to the British and as many as 13 villages were punished. After this event there was no armed conflict by the Nagas. In 1889 the Ao region was brought under British rule with the consent of the people who were tired of fighting and wanted British protection from the more war like tribe from across the Dikhu. For incorporating the rest of the territories of the eastern Angamis and the Sema Nagas the Deputy Commissioner was authorized to exercise political influence through his official tours and settling inter-tribal disputes and securing the consent to merge with British India. In this way, with the help of diplomacy and show of military power the Nagas were gradually won over who started attending markets and fairs and doing trade with the people in the plains. Police out-posts were established in all strategic places for the maintenance of law and order. The people started co-operating with the government and agreed to pay nominal revenue and to supply labour when required. Headmen of their communities were appointed in each village through whom government could reach to the people for all official purposes.

Incorporation of Lushai Hills

The Lushai Hills situated at the south of Surma valley and inhabited by various tribes known by the generic name of Kuki, made their first raid in 1849. They were the tribe who were well acquainted with the making of cartridges out of gun powder and possessed fire arms. Punitive expeditions were organized from time to time to deter them from this practice of raiding and looting the plains people. In 1871-72 two columns of the British force marched through the Lushai hills and successfully punished the wrong doers. In November 1849 the Lushais under the leadership of Vonpilal raided a Manipuri village named Rupchera, ten miles from Silchar where twenty-nine persons were killed and forty-two carried off. To punish the offenders Government of Bengal directed Colonel Lister, Commandant SLI to proceed immediately to deal against the aggressors. Accordingly, in early January 1850, Colonel Lister proceeded with 1000 of SLI and 150 armed Civil Police and on reaching the place launched a sudden attack on Mora, a large Lushai village with 800 houses, killed six people, destroyed the village and burned the granaries, taking advantage of the absence of the Lushai chief and his fighting men. The government established military out-posts at strategic places like Aijawl and Changsil in the northern portion of the hills and at Lungleh, in the southern part so as to prevent any further break-down of law and order. Political officers were posted at Aijawl and Lungleh to start preliminary administration. By this time it appeared that the Lushais have submitted themselves to the military power of the government and accepted the over-lordship of the British. There was no major insurgency in Lushai hills except one incident of the sudden murder by some miscreants of Captain Browne, Political officer, who was on his way without sufficient guard. The outbreak was suppressed immediately and the ringleaders were arrested and deported. The southern portion of the hill was at first administered by Bengal government and the northern portion by the Chief Commissioner of Assam but on 1st April, 1898 both the tracts were amalgamated into one and placed under the Chief Commissioner of Assam.

Integration of Manipur

The state of Manipur, inhabited by a warlike tribe called Meitei had been an independent state situated along side the Naga and Lushai Hills ever since prehistoric time. Manipur had been known throughout the ages by different names, as Meitrabak, Kangleipak or Meeteileipak while the Burmese called them Kathe, and the Ahoms, Meklee. It is stated that the past history of Manipur is merely legendary and not based on reliable evidence. The reliable part of the account begins only from 1714 onwards which is maintained in record by the kings of Ava. After the reign of Gharib Nawaz, Manipur passed on a period of internal war of what Mackenzie described as "the most savage revolting type in which sons murdered fathers, and brothers murdered brothers, without a single trait of heroism to relieve the dark scene of blood and treachery." A divided home is a divided power. Taking advantage of this royal family dispute the Burmese invaded Manipur several times and left it thoroughly plundered and rapined. In 1755 and 1758 the Burmese overran twice and a part of it was permanently annexed. In 1765 the Burmese invaded Manipur for the third time when the king Jai Singh was forced to flee to Cachar. After the death of Jai Singh in 1799 the state of Manipur plunged into the deep conspiracy and treason among his sons for the throne. The high drama of internal dispute continued until 1826 when the British appeared in the scene and settled down the dispute by restoring Gobinda Chandra to the throne of Cachar and Gambhir Singh as the king of Manipur who had himself been responsible for driving out the Burmese and because of this he had the better claim to the throne of Manipur than either of his brothers.

After having been reinstated as the Raja of Cachar, Gobinda Chandra acknowledged the allegiance to the East India Company by a treaty executed at Badarpur on the 6th March, 1824 and agreed to pay a tribute of Rs. 10,000 per year and to submit to the Company's arbitration in the case of disputes with other Rajas. The Company, on the other hand, undertook to protect him from external aggression, to leave him to manage his own internal affairs, and to make provision for the Manipuri princes who had lately occupied his country.[11] This is how the state of Manipur was formally integrated into the British Empire.

Subjugation of Small Chieftains

Gobinda Chandra, after having been reinstated as Raja of Cachar by the British, turned to be an oppressor. He started imposing heavy duties and many other unsparing exactions on his own people. He behaved most tyrannically towards the Manipuris who had settled in his territory. He also failed to pay the tribute to the government which he promised to pay as per Badarpur agreement of 1824. Thus he became so unpopular among his subjects that a conspiracy was hatched against him and eventually he was assassinated in 1830. He had no descendant, either lineal or adopted, to succeed to the throne for which the government annexed the portion of Cachar which belonged to him by a proclamation dated August 4, 1832.

The other half of Cachar was under the possession of one Tularam by way of claiming that he was the descendant of an ancient line of princes, anterior to that to which the late ruler had belonged. But this was, later on, proved to be false. Therefore, the government annexed his territory in 1854 and prevented him from using the title of Raja and was imposed with a tribute of four elephant tusks a year. He was also not permitted to deal with criminal cases other than petty offences. All criminal cases of serious nature were tried at the District Headquarters, Nowgong. On the annexation of Cachar it was formed into a district with its Headquarters at Silchar and was placed in charge of a Superintendent, who was subordinate to the Chief Commissioner of Assam.

The Chief of the Mataks who held the title of Bar Senapati, died in 1839. His second son, Maju Gohain succeeded him and claimed all the privileges enjoyed by his father but they were not given to him on the ground that the government had allowed these rights and privileges for the term of his life only. Apart from this Maju Gohain refused to accept the share of revenue at the scale originally proposed by David Scott. The offer was rejected by other members of the family too, whereupon the British representative, Captain Vetch assumed direct management of the entire Matak country. In 1842 a proclamation was issued announcing the incorporation of Matak and Sadiya into the British territory. Both these tracts were added to the Lakhimpur district, the headquarters of which was transferred to Dibrugarh.

The countries of the Daflas, Akas, Abors, Miris, Mishmis etc. bordering the extreme North Eastern frontiers of Assam were clubbed together to form a separate political division by the name, North East Frontier Tracts (NEFT) in 1914. Initially this tract was divided into two sections, viz. the Central and Eastern sections comprising the Dibrugarh Frontier Tract and some more areas in the south and the western section and each of the two sections were placed under one Political officer. In 1919 the Central and Eastern sections were called respectively the Lakhimpur Frontier Tract and the Sadiya Frontier Tract, while the western section was renamed as Balipara Frontier Tract. In 1937 all these three Frontier Tracts came to be considered as Excluded Areas of the Province of Assam under the provisions of the Government of India Act, 1935.

This is how the East India Company and later on the British government succeeded in annexing and consolidating its rule over the hills and plains of North East Frontier by the sheer use of military power and manoeuvering political diplomacy.

A careful reading of the facts enumerated in the preceding chapters will leave no room for doubt that behind the British victory against the Burmese and the consolidation of colonial rule in the entire North East Frontier, there was the powerful military organization. It can also be clearly seen that without the aid of the well-organised and trained soldiers, especially the redoubtable Gorkhas, the British would not have been able to penetrate into the hilly terrain and subjugate the refractory hill tribes in their mountain fastness. It was, at the first instance, the fighting skill, versatility and indomitable courage of the Gorkhas, on whom the British relied so much, and at the second instance, the familiarity with the topography and climate of the local recruits like the Manipuris, Cacharis, Jarvas etc. that accounted for the success in the whole campaign. Bampfylde Fuller, the Chief Commissioner of Assam, wrote – "The task of pacifying and humanizing these primitive hill people would have been impossible had there not been at the command of the civil government a trained and armed force which could be employed in small detachments, could be rapidly set in movement and could make shift with a minimum of transport."[12] With the help of these soldiers the British succeeded not only in expelling the Burmese from Assam but also in subjugating the hill tribes and establishing British paramountcy over the entire North East Frontier. It was hard to expel the formidable Burmese from the soil of Assam but it was even harder to establish the rule of law over the unruly primitive hill tribes and the heterogeneous Assamese people of the Brahmaputra valley which could be possible only with the help of military might and diplomacy.

At the advent of the British the condition of the people of Brahmaputra valley was extremely deplorable. The Ahom palace was embroiled in high treason and conspiracy among the princes each one vying for the throne. The government was divided and the Ahom army was simply unable either to stand against foreign invaders or to contend internal insurgency. The Burmese had been unleashing reign of terror by committing plunder and pillage while the Moamorias rebellion had taken upper hand and perpetrated untold atrocities on the people. They burnt down people's houses, destroyed their granaries leading to terrible famine, disease and death. The process of decay and fall of the Ahom kingdom had virtually started. Had the British not appeared at the scene, the history of Assam would have been a different one. To quote E.A. Gait – "It is impossible to say what would have been the ultimate fate of the unhappy Assamese had they been left unaided to the tender mercies of the Burmese."[13]

The British, with the help of military power, drove away the Burmese troops and compelled the king of Ava to sign the treaty of Yandaboo on the 24th February, 1826 agreeing to abstain from all interference in the affairs of Assam. Apart from freeing Brahmaputra valley from the Burmese, Govinda Chandra was restored to the throne of Cachar by the British. Gambhir Singh was helped to recover possession of Manipur and the Jaintia Raja Ram Singh was confirmed in his possession, both in the hills and the valleys of the north bank of Surma river. The British also subdued the rebellion of the Moamorias and put a stop to their inhuman oppression once for all. Gradually, peace and normalcy returned back in the Brahmaputra valley. For restoration of law and order and better administration David Scott was appointed as the Agent to the Governor General in 1823 and the whole region of Eastern Frontier — from Cachar and Sylhet in the south to the Sikkim in the north was placed under his jurisdiction. The territory of Sadiya, east of Dhansiri river was made over to Purandar Singh and made Raja of Upper Assam while the rest of Assam was divided into four districts, viz. Goalpara, Kamrup, Darrang and Nowgong. The territory of upper Assam under Purandar Singh was later on annexed to British administration in 1838 for mismanagement and default of revenue by Purandar Singh. Gauhati was made the Headquarters of the Commissioner of Assam. For the purpose of the administration of justice and control, civil, criminal and revenue courts were established in all the districts under the Act II of 1835. In 1874 the Assam region was separated from Bengal Presidency, Sylhet was added to it and its status was upgraded to a Chief Commissioner's Province. In the same year Shillong was made the capital of Assam. The Board of Revenue was established for major policy decisions regarding land and revenue matters. For the regulation of procedures in civil and criminal cases, set of rules were introduced in Assam Code in 1837. No special instructions were, however, laid down for the conduct of revenue business. According to the treaty signed on 12 August, 1765 the East India Company assumed the administration of Bengal, Bihar and Orissa through the grant of Diwani by the Mughal Emperor, Shah Alam II. This treaty brought the British into direct relations with the Garos, Khasis and the Jaintia Hills which situated contiguous to the revenue estates of Sherpur, Karoibari, Kalumalupara, Bholaganj and Theriaghat of north-east Bengal. Besides this revenue connections the British had special interest in the trade in limestone of Khasi Hills which proved to be lucrative business. The European traders had secured necessary permissions to work on the limestone quarries from the Khasi chiefs.

NOTES

1. W.J. Allen, p. 20, C.U. Aitchison, *A Collection of Treaties, Engagements and Sannads,* Vol. XII, 1931, p. 238.
2. *Ibid.*, p. 28, P.R.T. Gurdon, *The Khasis*, p. 75.
3. Hamlet Bareh, *History and Culture of The Khasis*, pp. 184-85.
4. *Ibid.*, p. 161.
5. *Ibid.*, p. 162.
6. *Ibid.*
7. *Ibid.*, p. 172.
8. B.J.P., 1815, 25 April, No. 17; Sisson to Bayley; Hamilton, W., *The Eastern Indian Gazetteer*, p. 567.
9. Colonel L.W. Shakespear, *The History of Assam Rifles*, p. 31.
10. C.U. Atchinson, Vol. II, 1872, p. 230.
11. E.A. Gait, *A History of Assam*, p. 341-42.
12. Colonel L.W. Shakespear, *op. cit.*, *Forewords*, pp. vii-viii.
13. E.A. Gait, *op. cit.*, p. 332.

6

Epilogue

The British annexation of Assam in 1826 marked the end of an era in the annals of Assam's history. It also closed the chapter of Ahom rule over Brahmaputra valley that lasted for nearly six centuries. The British rule that followed witnessed the beginning of the formation of a greater Assam comprising both the Brahmaputra and Surma valleys including the surrounding hill areas. The British not only expelled the Burmese from Assam but also liberated it from a state of dire anarchy, political intrigues and traumatic miseries of the Assamese people. During Ahom rule the royal court had become a hot-bed of conspiracies that involved constant internal squabbles and murder for power. The Moamoriahs had turned into open rebellion and seized the power of the government forcing the Ahom king Gaurinath Singh to flee for his life. The oppressions of the Ahom Kings drove them into rebellion and about 1770 AD they attacked, captured and succeeded in holding for nearly six months Gauhati, the capital of the Ahom kingdom.[1] The Moamoriahs were a sect of proselytes to Hinduism who denied the supremacy of the Brahmins and rejected the worship of Siva. Taking the advantage of political turmoil, the Burmese had overrun the country unleashing a reign of terror, with barbaric plunder, kidnapping and murder. "Thirty thousand Assamese had been carried off as slaves by the Burmese. Many thousands had lost their lives and large tracts of country been laid desolate by the wars, famines and pestilences."[2] At such critical juncture the British emerged as the messiah, the savior of Assam. On the desperate appeal made by the Ahom king, Gourinath Singh Lord Cornwallis ordered a detachment of sepoys under Captain Welse who completely routed the Moamoriahs and other rebellious Chiefs in the cold season of 1792-93. Subsequently in 1826 the British troops expelled the

Burmese from the Brahmaputra valley, quelled the Moamoriah rebellion, and subdued the war like hill tribes and brought back peace and order not only in the Brahmaputra valley but also in the entire North East Frontier including the hill areas and forged a unification of a greater Assam. Manipur was restored back to Gambhir Singh, the Jaintia Raja, Ram Singh, was confirmed in his possessions both in the hills and the plain belts of Surma valley and Govind Chandra was reinstated as the Raja of Cachar. Historian H.K. Borpujari termed this act of the British East India Company as "divine dispensation".

> The horrors of Burmese invasion and the depredations of neighbouring hill tribes were still fresh in their minds to think of any other rule than the British which alone stood for peace and order and which was to them a divine dispensation."[3]

Pacifying and taming the hill tribes and bringing them all under one consolidated British rule was, however, not an easy task. It involved resorting to strong military action and prolonged punitive expeditions, political diplomacy and consistent pacifying and civilizing efforts. In this crusade, as referred to by the Chief Commissioner of Assam, the Gorkha Regiments and a few other local forces played the major role. Bampfylde Fuller, the Chief Commissioner of Assam stated as follows:[4]

> "It was fortunate for the government of the province that on these emergent occasions it could rely upon a garrison of regular troops that include the Gorkha Regiments."

Thus the Gorkha regiment was the central force in the whole operation of expelling the Burmese from Assam, quelling the Moamorias to save the Assamese people from oppression and establishing peace and order among the infighting hill tribes.

The garrison of regular troops referred to above by the Chief Commissioner of Assam consisted of the 1st Assam Light Infantry, the 2nd Assam Light Infantry, the Sylhet Light Infantry and the Bengal Infantry Battalion. These regular forces were raised at various places at different times, and were composed of the Hindustanis, Manipuris, the Gorkhas and the local Jarvas. The class composition of these forces, however, kept on changing as the time passed on, depending upon their suitability according to the climate and topography of Assam hill areas. In course of time the services of the Hindustanis and the Manipuris not being found suitable, their numbers were gradually reduced in favour of the Gorkhas and the Jarvas and, in the long run, the Gorkhas were preferred to be the best soldiers in all aspects of their services.

In the Gorkhas the British found the right material who could withstand the inhospitable climate and the hilly terrain of Assam which was absent in the Hindustani soldiers. At the same time, the Gorkhas possessed the much needed striking power with abundant courage and fighting skill which were lacking in the local levies raised in Assam. Captain John Bryan Neufville, the Commanding Officer and Political Agent for Upper Assam had always preferred Gorkhas for hill and jungle situation of Assam. Accordingly he was allowed to raise two companies of Gorkhas from the draft of Champaran and Dinajpur battalions. Captain Neufville was all praise about the Gorkhas. He said, they were –

> "Proverbially brave, active and capable of enduring fatigue both in the hills and jungles and free from the prejudices which the Hindus of the regular troops were invariably accustomed."[5]

Captain G.E. Westmacott in his *Notes on the History of Assam* expressed the view on Gorkhas as follows:[6]

> "The Gorkhas are a noble set of fellows distinguished by some of the virtues and stained also by a few of the vices peculiar to Europeans. Unlike the natives of Hindustan they do not yield themselves up to the demoralising custom of Assamese of taking large quantities of opium and maintaining on the establishment a plurality of women."

The Jarvas of Lower Assam (a mixed group of the Rabhas, Kacharis and Hajongs), who under David Scott had established their reputation in the malarial jungles of the Garo Duars, was now being put forward as another source of recruits.[7] The Manipuris who were once considered as the best soldiers, after having been suspected of their integrity, were replaced by Gorkhas towards the middle of 1830. The Manipuris were suspected to be connected in the assassination of Raja Govinda Chandra of Cachar in which Raja Gambhir Singh of Manipur was involved. The Government of British India having been convinced of the suspicion attached to the Manipuris had agreed to gradual induction of Gorkhas into the battalion.[8] The Gorkha recruitment, therefore, picked up swiftly and by the year 1870 the British began to enlist Gorkhas in increasing numbers.

From 1875 onwards the Frontier Police came to be re-organized on a better footing by gradually increasing its quality and strength. Till 1875 the total strength of Assam Frontier Police was 24000 all ranks which was raised to 33000 by the end of 1882. Earlier, in 1879 a separate force of Frontier Police of 3000 strong was raised with Gorkha recruits and posted at Tura, Garo Hills. In 1885 each of the units was given two 6-pounder mountain guns, which in 1903 were handed over to the Military Police battalions.[9]

In the early days the Cachar Levy was carrying weapon, a sword attached to the belt which impeded the sepoy's progress through the jungle, therefore, in 1865 the more useful '*Khukri*' was substituted in its place. Ever since that time *khukri*, the Gorkhas national weapon, came to be used in all military organizations of Assam as versatile instrument to be used in both war and peace. In 1882 the Assam Frontier Police was re-organised and given the title of Assam Military Police, and we find three new Military Police Battalions, the Naga Hills Police Battalion, Lakhimpur Police Battalion and the Surma Valley Police Battalion. These three full-strength Battalions were given to wear distinctive silver buttons and cap badges with two crossed-*khukris* on each shoulder strap.[10] This measure taken by the government was in conformity with the priorities given to Gorkha recruits in the Military Police. It was also hoped that the use of versatile Gorkha *khukri* and wearing the badge with crossed-*khukri* would provide a sense of pride and strength to the psyche of the recruits besides looking smarter. These battalions were also given the service of a European Sergeant deputed from a British regiment to assist the Commandants in imparting drill and discipline. During that time, the class composition of the Military Police Battalions, according to Colonel Shakespear, had risen to three-fourths the strength of Gorkhas and one-fourth of Jarvas or as near that as possible.[11] The recruitment for some time was tried with Sikhs, Punjabis, Dogras and to a small extent with Mohammedans. The two former classes not answering well in Assam situation their recruitment was stopped after a few years, but the Dogras continued to be recruited until about 1912 by the Naga Hills Military Police. Eventually, the composition of each battalion came to be three-fourths of the Gorkhas and one-fourth of Jarvas or as near as possible.[12]

While there was a high demand for Gorkha recruits, the Nepal Durbar was not willing to allow its subjects to join Indian army or other forces in Assam. On the issue of Gorkha recruitment Jang Bahadur, the Prime Minister of Nepal was strictly non-committal. He never agreed with the British nor frankly be excused for fear of displeasure of the British and always kept himself aloof. Inside the country he took stringent measures against the Nepalese leaving the country without authority of the Durbar. None could go beyond Noakot and cross the Trisuliganga without passport issued by the Durbar. The Gorkhas who were already in the Indian Army were not allowed to re-enter Nepal to meet their family except when they had taken discharge from British services. Jang Bahadur's fear was that the Gorkhas serving in Indian Army would be used as agencies through whom the British government would smuggle out new Gorkha recruits.[13] The British Resident to Nepal, Ramsay ruefully wrote in his report to the Government as follows:

> "The Durbar is, and always has been, averse to its subjects entering the British service and orders have long existed to prevent their doing so without the Minister's previous permission; and a few years ago Maharaj Jung Bahadur went so far as to declare that no Sepahees in the British army, natives of Nepal, 'on leaves only from their regiments', should be allowed to re-enter the country and visit their families, an order which he only withdrew after I had strongly remonstrated against it."[14]

The process of Gorkha recruitment became easier only after the Agreement of Mutual Concession was signed between the Government of India and Nepal Durbar in 1885. The Nepalese Government was in urgent need of arms and ammunitions from India for the impending war against Tibet while British needed Gorkha recruits for immediate expansion of Indian Army. Nepal had already established a factory of making snider cartridge and she needed copper and chemicals from India for the factory. It was, therefore, considered a wise deal to comply with Nepal's request for supply of arms and to obtain Gorkha recruits in exchange. After some negotiations the deal was finally settled. Ranuddip Singh, the Prime Minister of Nepal agreed to supply 5600 Gorkhas annually to India while Lord Dufferin, the Viceroy of India agreed to give to Nepal one rifle for each Gorkha recruit and also to allow facilities to import copper sheets and chemicals for manufacture of ammunitions.

General Frederick Roberts who graded Gorkhas as martial class was happy to get enough Gorkhas for his Indian Army. He organized a systematic recruiting programme by opening a number of recruiting depots at Darjeeling, Pilibhit, Gorakhpur and Bahraich. Recruiting parties composed of experienced Gorkha officers were appointed whose initiative and resourcefulness enabled them to procure good number of recruits. By the end of 1886 Roberts raised three new Gorkha battalions in addition to strengthening the existing battalions. The Sixth Gorkha Rifles came into existence in 1864 by the name of 42nd Bengal Infantry (Gorkha) formed out of the Cuttack Legion which was raised as back as 1817. This regiment was finally given its present name of 6th Gorkha Rifles in 1903. In the same year of 1903 another two regiments, viz. 7th and 8th Gorkha Rifles were christened both of them having their origin in Assam. The former had its genesis in the Assam Light Infantry, raised in Assam in 1835, while the latter originated from the 16th Sylhet Local Battalion which was raised on February 9, 1828. The 8th Gorkha Rifles, since its inception, had its headquarters at Shillong till 1934 and was busy in the affairs of the hills of Assam and earned the reputation as "Jungle Barshers" while engaged in Manipur warfare.

After the Gorakhpur recruiting depot was opened the best recruits from Magar and Gurung community were available but during Afghan war (1879-80) the Government of India restricted recruitment of Rai, Limbu, Magar and Gurung into Assam Military Police due to their demand for regular Indian army. This had an adverse effect on the enrolment of Assam Military Police and recourse was taken to trying for more Cacharis and Jarvas, however, without much success. Ultimately, the situation was resolved in 1891 when a new Recruiting Depot was opened at Purnia, the feet of Darjeeling Hills for recruitment of Gorkhas at source. After a few years this depot was shifted to Darjeeling itself. Thus, Assam continued to recruit a good number of Gorkhas from Darjeeling recruiting depot and other sources. The Gorakhpur depot became exclusively reserved for the Indian army while the Darjeeling depot was free for Assam's requirement.

In 1914 the fourth battalion of the Assam Military Police was raised and named Darrang Military Police Battalion. In this year the government introduced uniformity of class composition for all the four Military Police battalions and the ratio was fixed at 50 per cent or 4 companies of Gorkhas and 50 per cent of Jarvas and Dogras combined together in equal proportion.[15] The Dogra element was introduced in Assam Military Police following the shortage of recruits as a result of restriction imposed by Indian army in enlisting martial class Gorkhas.

In the wake of the First World War in 1914 the Assam Military Police was asked to send drafts to the Gorkha Regiments in various theatres of operations. The first draft was dispatched to the 3rd and the 8th Gorkha Rifles on 18 October, 1914 which consisted of three Havildars and 100 sepoys. After this the process of sending drafts continued till the end of the war during which period all the four MP Battalions sent selected officers and sepoys to join the Gorkha Regiments in France, Egypt, Gallipoli, Mesopotamia etc. Those sent between October 1914 and April 1917 totalled 5 Officers, and 649 of all ranks some of whom served with the 2nd Gorkha Rifles, others with 3rd, 6th, 7th, 8th, and 10th Gorkha Rifles.[16] The majority of those who went were Gorkhas and they all acquitted themselves well in the war which is evident from the letters of appreciation sent by the Officers Commanding of the Gorkha Rifles where they served and the medal tally won by them. The O.C. of 1/10 Gorkha Rifles, in his letter of appreciation No. AF/2/13 of 29.3.22 addressed to the I.G.P. Shillong wrote:

> The draft of the Assam Rifles did splendid work throughout the whole of the four years they served in Mesopotamia with the unit under my command. Two of the draft obtained the IDSM for bravery in the field, viz. No.734 Havildar Chandra Singh Chettri for gallantry in action during the Arab rebellion of 1920, and No.1076 Rifleman Karna Bahadur Chetrum for gallantry at the battle of Kala Shergat in 1918."[17]

The GOC, 8th, Lucknow Division, General May, remarked – "I was greatly pleased with all the work I saw carried out."[18]

In recognition of the excellent services rendered in the Great War by the men of the Assam Military Police Battalions, the Government of India, in 1917, sanctioned the old title to be changed to that of 'Assam Rifles'. The four Military Police Battalions became serially, the 1st to 4th Battalions of Assam Rifles. In the year 1920 a new 5th Battalion was raised to which 4 Gorkha officers and 82 rifles were transferred as a nucleus for this battalion. In the year 1925 the Government of India by a notification, permanently affiliated the Assam Rifles to the Gorkha Regimental group of the Indian Army as mentioned below:

Details of the Affiliation of Battalions of the Assam Rifles with Gorkha Infantry Groups of the Indian Army

1st (Lushai Hills) Battalion to the 2nd Gorkha Group	- (2nd and 9th G.R)
2nd (Lakhimpur) Battalion to the 5th Gorkha Group	- (7th and 10th G.R.)
3rd (Naga Hills) Battalions to the 1st Gorkha Group	- (1st and 4th G.R.)
4th Battalion to the 4th Gorkha Group	- (5th and 6th G.R.)
5th Battalion to the 3rd Gorkha Group	- (3rd and 8th G.R.)

Assam continued to recruit Gorkhas, as their number in Assam Rifles increased by leaps and bounds. The following table facilitates a comparative reading of the relative strength of Gorkhas in relation to other communities of Assam in all the five battalions of the Assam Rifles in 1922.

Battalions	*Gorkhas Jarvas*	*others*	*Total*	*Gorkha*	*Per cent*
1st Battalion	762	48	42	852	89.44
2nd Battalion	647	137	10	794	81.48
3rd Battalion	592	166	73	831	71.24
4th Battalion	614	108	81	823	79.60
5th Battalion	552	200	41	793	69.60
Grand Total	**3194**			**4093**	**78.00**

The figures stated in above Table show the predominance of Gorkhas by overwhelming percentage over other communities in all the five Battalions of the Assam Rifles. Looking at the total recruits of all the five battalions it will appear that out of the total of 4093 recruits the Gorkhas were 3194 and their percentage was 78 per cent over all other classes which was the highest.

In 1929 when Assam Rifles Manual was prepared the ideal class composition was fixed as follows:

Battalions	*Gorkhas*	*Jarvas*	*Lushais*	*Nagas*	*Kukis*
1st Battalion	50%	37.5%	12.5%	–	–
2nd Battalion	62.5%	37.5%	–	–	–
3rd Battalion	50%	37.5%	–	12.5%	–
4th Battalion	50.5%	37.5%	–	–	12.5%
5th Battalion	50%	50%	–	–	–

This ratio of class composition remained unchanged till the British left India in 1947.

After India's Independence the Assam Rifles rapidly expanded in its strength and scope by raising more battalions and widening its power and function so as to become a cohesive organization for the broader nation building objective of the country. Earlier Assam Rifles was placed under the civil police with the Inspector General of Police as its head. After Independence it was made an independent body with its own Director General. The rank of the Commanding Officer of Assam Rifles was also upgraded to that of the Lieutenant General who was deputed from the regular Indian Army.

> The role of the Assam Rifles was fairly widened by involving it into the task of rescue and relief operation during natural calamities like flood havoc, earthquake etc. and also for helping the civil administration in maintenance of peace and order during political uprisings. During the earthquake of 1950, the Assam Rifles jawans rendered excellent service in relief and rehabilitation works. After the earthquake Assam has been suffering from flash flood of Brahmaputra river almost every year which inundated vast areas of standing

> crops and render thousands of people homeless. It is the Assam Rifles which is handy to be pressed into service in helping the civil authorities in providing relief and rescue operation to the affected people.

Before 1962 the Assam Rifles jawans, together with regular army jawans, were detailed to guard Indian posts in far-flung Indo-Tibetan borders along Arunachal Pradesh. During Chinese aggression of 1962 the Chinese troops launched a massive attack with machine guns and artilleries and blew up the Indian Posts. The Platoon Commander, Som Bahadur and his 20 men of Assam Rifles went down fighting bravely. Many other Assam Rifles jawans detailed at other Indian posts also lost their lives.

> The Assam Rifles is also engaged in anti-insurgency duties. Ever since 1956 when the Naga insurgents declared Nagaland as 'Naga sovereign state' and hoisted their state flag at village Phensia, till to this day, the whole of the North Eastern region including Assam has been the hot-bed of political insurgency and militancy. During this long period of more than six decades the Assam Rifles together with other Central military forces are in the thick of the herculean task of countering insurgency and keeping peace and order in the North East. With the passage of time the strength of Assam Rifles has been enhanced considerably for making it fit and effective in service. In 1960 there were 17 battalions which were increased to 21 in 1968, and today there are 46 battalions spread all over the North Eastern states with Headquarters at several places. It has one Training Centre with the capacity of training 1800 recruits at a time and a number of Logistic Units.

Assam Rifles is, today, no longer a military organization but a 'sentinel of the North East', an effective and trained set of tools in the hands of civil authority. Dr. Verrier Elwin, an eminent Anthropologist and Adviser to the Government of India, Tribal Areas of North East, rightly said, "Assam Rifles is the custodian of law and order, pioneers of every advance into interior, the guardians on the borders and, above all, the friends of the hill people."

Let us not, however, forget the fact that this great institution called Assam Rifles is not a creation of Indian Government but a legacy of the British India. The Assam Rifles has its genesis in the 'Cachar Levy' a humble militia raised by Captain Grange with a strength of 750 strong all ranks. This tiny military organization, before the British handed it over to India, underwent numerous experiments, research and developments, changed in form and class compositions and rose from strength to strength until it became a time tested, matured and a strong para-military force.

NOTES

1. Alexander Mackenzie, *The North East Frontier of India*, Mittal Publications, Delhi, reprint 1999, p. 3.
2. *Ibid.*, p. 7.
3. H.K. Borpujari, *The Comprehensive History of Assam*, Vol. IV, Guwahati, 1992.
4. L.W. Shakespear, *History of Assam Rifles*, London, 1929.
5. FSC. 10 November, 1826: Nos. 21-22.
6. Captain G.E. Westmacott, "Notes on the History of Assam", Ms 2217/3 Aberdin University, Scotland. By kind permission of Prof. Imdad Hussain.
7. Imdad Hussain, "Soldiers and Settlers: Recruitment of Gorkhas," in The Nepalis in North East India, edt. By A.C. Sinha and T.B. Subba.
8. *Ibid.*, p. 72.
9. Col. L.W. Shakespear, *op. cit.*, p. 7.
10. *Ibid.*, p. 56.
11. *Ibid.*, p. 57.
12. *Ibid.*
13. K.K. Muktan, *The Legendary Gorkhas*, 2002, p. 54.
14. Ramsay to Secretary to the Government of India, in the Foreign Department, Simla, No. 18, June 1866.
15. HPA, April 1915: Nos. 73-92, September 1915: Nos. 44-45. Note by J.H. Wheeler.
16. Col. L.W. Shakespear, *op. cit.*, p. 202.
17. Appendix C of *History of Assam Rifles* by Col. L.W. Shakespear, p. 286.
18. *Ibid.*, p. 196.

7

Progressive Title Changes in Gurkha Infantry While in British Service*

1st Gurkha Rifles

1815 1st Nasiri Battalion; 1823 5th, 6th, or 1st Nasiri Local Battalion; 1826 4th, or Nasiri Local Battalion; 1843 4th, or Nasiri (Rifle Battalion); 1850 66th or Goorkha Regiment, Bengal Native Infantry; 1858 66th or Goorkha Light Infantory Regiment, Bengal Native Infantry; 1861 11th Regiment of Bengal Native Infantry; 1861 1st Goorkha Regiment (Light Infantry); 1886 1st Goorkha Regiment (Light Infantry); 1891 1st Gurkha (Rifle) Regiment; 1901 1st Gurkha Rifles; 1903 1st Gurkha Rifles (the Malaum Regiment); 1906 1st Prince of Wales Own Gurkha Rifles; 1910 1st King George's Own Gurkha Rifles (the Malaun Regiment);.1937 1st King George V's Own Gurkha Rifles (the Malaun Regiment); 1947 left the British service.

2nd Gurkha Rifles

1815 Sirmoor Battalion; 1823 8th (or Sirmoor) Local Battalion; 1826 6th (or Sirmoor) Local Battalion; 1850 Sirmoor Battalion; 1858 Sirmoor Rifle Regiment; 1861 17th Regiment of Bengal Native Infantry; 1861 2nd Goorkha Regiment; 1864 2nd Goorkha (the Sirmoor Rifles) Regiment; 1876 2nd (Prince of Wales's Own) Goorkha Regiment (the Sirmoor Rifles); 1886 2nd (the Prince of Wales's Own) Goorkha Regiment (The Sirmoor Rifles); 1891 2nd

* Byron Farwell, *The Gurkhas,* (London, 1984), pp. 256 ff.

(the Prince of Wales's Own) Gurkha (Rifles); Regiment (the Sirmoor Rifles); 1901 2nd (the Prince of Wales's Own) Gurkha Rifles (the Sirmoor Rifles); 1906 2nd King Edward's Own Gurkha Rifles (the Sirmoor Rifles); 1936 2nd King Edward VII's Own Gurkha Rifles (the Sirmoor Rifles); 1947 to British Army.

3rd Gurkha Rifles

1815 Kumaon Battalion; 1816 Kumaon Provincial Battalion; 1823 9th (or Kumaon) Local Battalion; 1826 7th (or Kumaon) Local Battalion; 1860 Kumaon Battalion; 1861 18th Regiment of Bengal Native Infantry; 1861 3rd Goorkha Regiment; 1864 3rd (the Kumaon) Goorkha Regiment; 1887 3rd Goorkha Regiment; 1891 3rd Goorkha (Rifle) Regiment; 1901 3rd Gurkha Rifles; 1907 3rd The Queen's Own Gurkha Rifles; 1908 3rd Queen Alexandra's Own Gurkha Rifles; 1947 left the British service.

4th Gurkha Rifles

1857 Extra Goorkha Regiment; 1861 19th Regiment of Bengal Native Infantry; 1861 4th Goorkha Regiment; 1891 4th Gurkha (Rifle) Regiment; 1901 4th Gurkha Rifles; 1924 4th Prince of Wales's Own Gurkha Rifles; 1947 left the British service.

5th Gurkha Rifles

1858 25th Punjab Infantry, or Hazara Goorkha Battalion; 1861 7th Regiment of Infantry (or Hazara Goorkha Battalion), Punjab Irregular Force; 1861 5th Goorkha Regiment, the Hazara Goorkha Battalion; 1886 5th Goorkha Regiment, the Hazara Goorkha Battalion; 1887 5th Goorkha Regiment; 1891 5th Gurkha (Rifle) Regiment; 1901 5th Gurkha Rifles; 1903 5th Gurkha Rifles (Frontier Force); 1923 5th Royal Gurkha Rifles (Frontier Force); 1947 left the British service.

6th Gurkha Rifles

1817 Cuttack Legion; 1823 Rangpur Light Infantry Battalion; 1826 8th (or Rangpur) Local Light Infantry Battalion; 1828 8th (or Assam) Local Light Infantry Battalion; 1844 1st Assam Light Infantry; 1861

42nd Regiment of Bengal Native Infantry; 1864 42nd (Assam) Regiment of Bengal Native (Light) Infantry; 1885 42nd (Assam) Regiment of Bengal (Light) Infantry; 1886 42nd Regiment Goorkha Light Infantry; 1889 42nd (Goorkha) Regiment of Bengal (Light) Infantry; 1891 42nd Gurkha (Rifle) Regiment of Bengal Infantry; 1901 42nd Gurkha Rifles; 1903 6th Gurkha Rifles; 1947 to British Army; 1859 6th Queen Elizabeth's Own Gurkha Rifles.

7th Gurkha Rifles

1902 8th Gurkha Rifles; 1903 2nd Battalion, 10th Gurkha Rifles; 1907 7th Gurkha Rifles; 1947 to British Army; 1 January 1959 7th Duke of Edinburgh's Own Gurkha Rifles.

8th Gurkha Rifles

1824 16th or Sylhet Local Battalion; 1826 11 th or Sylhet Local (Light) Infantry Battalion; 1861' 48th Regiment of Bengal Native Infantry; 1861 44th Regiment of Bengal Native Infantry; 1864 44th (Sylhet) Regiment of Bengal Native (Light) Infantry; 1885 44th (Sylhet) Regiment of Bengal (Light) Infantry; 1886 44th Regiment, Goorkha (Light) Infantry; 1889 44th (Goorkha) Regiment Bengal (Light) Infantry; 1891 44th Gurkha (Rifle) Regiment of Bengal Infantry; 1901 44th Gurkha Rifles; 1903 8th Gurkha Rifles; 1907 became the 1st Battlion. 2nd Battalion raised at Gauhati: 1835 Assam Sebundy Corps; 1839 Lower Assam Sebundy Corps; 1839 1st Assam Sebundy Corps; 1844 2nd Assam Light Infantry; 1861 47th Regiment of Bengal Native Infantry; 1861 43rd Regiment of Bengal Native Infantry; 1884 43rd (Assam) Regiment of Bengal Native (Light) Infantry; 1865 43rd (Assam) Regiment of Bengal (Light Infantry; 1886 43rd Regiment Goorkha Light Infantry; 1889 43rd (Goorkha) Regiment of Bengal (Light) Infantry; 1891 43rd Gurkha (Rifle) Regiment of Bengal Infantry; 1901 43rd Gurkha Rifles; 1903 7th Gurkha Rifles; 1907 became the 2nd Battalion, 8th Gurkha Rifles; 1947 left the British service.

9th Gurkha Rifles

1817 Fatehgarh Levy; 1819 Manipuri Levy; 1823 1st Battalion. 32nd

Regiment of Bengal Native Infantry; 1824 63rd Regiment of Bengal Native Infantry; 1861 9th Regiment of Bengal Native Infantry; 1885 9th Regiment of Bengal Infantry; 1894 9th (Gurkha Rifles) Regiment of Bengal Infantry; 1901 9th Gurkha Rifles; 1947 left the British service.

10th Gurkha Rifles

1890 1st Regiment of Burma Infantry; 1891 10th Regiment (1st Burma Battalion) of Madras Infantry; 1892 10th Regiment (1st Burma Rifles) Madras Infantry; 1895 10th Regiment (1st Burma Gurkha Rifles) Madras Infantry; 1901 10th Gurkha Rifles; 1947 to British Army; 1949 10th Princess Mary's Own Gurkha Rifles.

Appendices

Appendix I

Affiliation of the Assam Rifles with the Gurkha Infantry Groups of the Indian Army

It has been decided, on the recommendation of the Government of Assam, that the Battalions of the Assam Rifles shall be affiliated to Gurkha Groups of the Indian Army. The affiliation will not in any respect affect the status of the Assam Rifles as a Military Police Force under the control of the Government of Assam.

2. In pursuance of the arrangement above described, it has been decided that:

(I) The battalions of the Assam Rifles shall be affiliated to the Gurkha Groups as detailed in the appendix to this Instruction.

(II) The British Officers of the battalions of the Assam Rifles shall be selected, as far as possible, from the Gurkha groups to which the battalions are affiliated, subject to the approval of the General Officer Commanding-in-Chief concerned, and of Army Headquarters, India.

(III) A party consisting of 1 Indian Officer, 2 Havildars, and 4 Naiks from each battalion of the Assam Rifles shall be attached for training annually to one of the four battalions of the parent Group; such attachment not to exceed a period of six months in any one year.

(IV) The Commandant and the Subadar-Major of the Gurkha battalion to which the party referred to in III above is attached for training may, subject to the sanction of the local military authorities, visit the affiliated battalion of the Assam Rifles during the year in which the training takes place, the cost involved by the visit being borne by the Government of Assam.

3. All other expenditures in connection with the scheme for the affiliation of the Assam Rifles to Gurkha Groups of the Indian Army will also be debitable to the Government of Assam.

Appendix to Army Instruction (India), No. 213 of 1925

Details of the affiliation of battalions of the Assam Rifles with Gurkha Infantry groups of the Indian Army.

1st (Lushai Hills) Battalion to the 2nd Gurkha Group (2nd and 9th Gurkha Rifles).
2nd (Lakhimpur) Battalion to the 5th Gurkha Group (7th and 10th Gurkha Rifles).
3rd (Naga Hills) Battalions to the 1st Gurkha Group (1st and 4th Gurkha Rifles).
4th Battalion to the 4th Gurkha Group (5th and 6th Gurkha Rifles).
5th Battalion to the 3rd Gurkha Group (3rd and 8th Gurkha Rifles).

Appendix II

Honours and Rewards gained by the Assam Rifles since 1891

1891	Subadar Sangram Sing	Indian Order of Merit—South Lushai Hills rising.
	Havildar Chandra Sing Thapa	
1894	Havildar Major Bakshi Ram	Order of Merit—Abor Expedition.
	Havildar Bhuta Sing	
1897	Subadar Major Jitman Gurung	Title of "Rai Bahadur."
1907	Subadar Major Arjan Rai	Title of "Sirdar Bahadur," also awarded the I.D.S.M. and King's Police Medal, and later Order of British India, 2nd Class.
1912	Jemadar Harka Sing Rai	I.D.S.M., Chinlong Expedition.
1912	Captain G.S. Dunbar, Sergt. Dorward, Subadar Jangbir Lama, and Jemadar Sarahjit Thapa were mentioned in despatches	Abor Expedition.
	Subadar Jangbir Lama Havildar Dalbahadar Thapa	I.D.S.M.
1913	Captain A. Graham	K.P.M., Daphla Expedition.
	Subadar Sanjai Subha	Order of British India, 2nd Class, and later the title of "Bahadur."
1914	Major C. Bliss	C.I.E., K.P.M.
	Subadar Major Jamaluddin Subadar Hari Ram	K.P.M. (King's Police Medal)
1915	Subadar Major Jamaluddin	Order of British India, 2nd Class, and later the title of "Khan Bahadur."
	Captain Montifiore	O.B.E., Chin Hills rising.

(*Contd.*)

	Subadar Hari Ram	I.D.S.M. Kuki operations.
	Subadar Nain Sing Mal	
1917 to 1919	Jemadar Hanspal Limbu	
	Rifleman Kishenbahadur Chettrie	
	Havildar Jangbir Gurung	
	Rifleman Bhabajit Rai	
	Subadar Pokul Thapa	K.P.M., Kuki operations.
	Also 6 Riflemen specialty promoted in the field, numerous "mentions" in despatches and a number of Jangi Inams were granted for these operations. Ten Indian officers and 22 other ranks also received various honours for the Kuki operations.	
1915 to 1920	Eleven Indian officers and 131 other ranks were specially promoted on the field, and 7 Indian officers and 69 other ranks were awarded various honours, including 7 I.O.M, 5 I.D.S.M., 12 M.S.M.	The Great War
1920	Subadar Major Hetma Rai	The title of "Rai Bahadur."
	Subadar Birman Thapa	I.D.S.M.
	Jemadar Satal Sing Cachari	
1921	Colonel L.W. Shakespear	C.B., C.I.E., Kuki Operations.
1924	Subadar Major Jangbir Lama	The title of "Sirdar Bahadur."
	Jemadar Surbir Ale	K.M.P., Rampa State Rebelion
	Subadar Kainbir Limbu	
	Subadar Kainbir Limbu	
	Subadar Major Mansur Rai	I.O.M.

Appendix III

Proceedings of the Chief Commissioner of Assam, Military Department, Shillong, April 1889

Formation of a Gurkha Village near Shillong. No. 8, Dated Camp, The 23rd January, 1889.

From

Brigadier-General Sir F.B. Norman, K.C.B., Commanding Assam District

To

The Secretary to the Chief Commissioner of Assam

The hardships, difficulties, and expense connected with the moving from one station to another in this province of the women and children of the three Gurkha Light Infantry Regiments, consequent either on the movement of the regiments in relief or the necessity of establishing a depot, should the regiment have been ordered on service, have been recently forcibly brought to my notice.

2. The numbers of women and children in these regiments is as follows: 42nd GLI, 170 women, 163 children; 43rd GLI, 130 women and 135 children; 44th GLI, 105 women and 126 children. As there is no limit to the number of men who may marry, these figures may be looked upon as the minimum number of women and children for whom it would be necessary to provide accommodation.

3. I have discussed the question with Colonel Evans, Commanding 43rd GLI, and he has consulted with the Native Officers of the regiment on the subject, and the result is embodied in Colonel Evans' Letter No. 1C, of the 14th instant, a copy of which is annexed. From this it will be seen that it is proposed to form a Gurkha village in the Khasi Hills for each regiment, where the women and children could remain when the regiment was not at Shillong. In these villages the pensioners and reserve men of the regiment would also reside. The details of the scheme would have to be worked out; but I should be glad to know whether it would be possible to provide land for the

proposed villages, I am aware that the land in the vicinity of Shillong is private property, and would have to be purchased; but if the price were not high, it would be to the advantage of the State to incur the expenditure, which would be a final cost. It would be preferable that the proposed villages should be near Shillong, rather than in the Jowai sub-division.

Appendix IV

In Memory of Hony Capt Kalu Thapa O.B.I. S.B., 44th Gurkha Rifles Enlisted in the 11th SYLHET Light Infantry in Jan 1858

Become sub maj in 1890 and proceed on pension on the 5th of Feb 1897 after 39 years faithful service granted the honorary rank of captain three years after retirement. Twice awarded the O.B.I. firstly the 2nd class in 1885 & later the 1st class of this order in 1895. He also received the Kaiser-i-hind-medal in 1877 and the coronation Delhi durbar medal in 1911, he received. The following medal and clasp for service in the field. Indian general service medal with clasp for service in Bhutan 1965, clasp for Lushai hills 1871, Clasp for Bhutan 1885, clasp for Bhutan 1887-1888, Clasp for Manipur (on frontier) 1891.

Died in Shillong on the 14th May, 1934; aged 94 years.

Appendix V

Copies of some of the letters from various Commanding Officers of Goorkha Regiments to whom the Assam Rifles sent reinforcements during the Great War between January 1915 and the end of 1918, and which show the value of their services during that period.

Copy of letter, No. 123/108/A, of 9th August, 1921, from the O.C. 1st K.G.O. Goorkha Rifles to the I.G.P. Shillong.

"I am very glad to take this opportunity of expressing on behalf of this Regt its high appreciation of the services of the men of the Assam Military Police who served with it from January 1915 to October 1918 in three theatres of war—*viz.* France, Mesopotamia, and Palestine, and who helped to maintain and enhance the reputation of the 1st K.G.O. Goorkha Rifles. I can assure you that their services were at all times of the most willing, their bravery and devotion to duty of the highest order, and to give them high compliment they fell at once into the order and discipline of this Regt as if to the manner born. We would have been disappointed with anything else from Goorkhas among their brother Goorkhas.

"In all, 1 Jemadar, 2 N.C.O.'s, and 156 Riflemen of the Assam Military Police served with us, of whom 14 were killed and 44 wounded. There were several promotions for gallantry and for deserving work, and they have themselves largely to thank for the fact that while with this Regt they were treated and regarded as 1st Goorkhas.

"I would be grateful if the men of the A.M.P. (especially those of the 2nd A.R.) still serving may be informed of our high appreciation of their work, and also that if at any future time of great stress their services be again lent, the reputation secured by their relations in the Great War will ensure them a hearty welcome with us."

Copy of letter, No. 2639/47/E, of August 9th, 1921, from the O.C. 2nd K.E.O. Goorkhas to the I.G.P. Shillong.

"Two drafts of the Assam Military Police joined this Regt. in France early in 1915. The first was a party of 1 Indian Officer (Subadar

Mansur Rai) and 900 other ranks of the Aijal Battn (Ist A.R.). They arrived at the Depot in Dehra Doon as early as November 1914. A second draft under Jemadar Bakhatman Gurung joined us in April 1915 in France after training with 1/7th G.R. at Quetta and consisted mainly of men from the Naga Hills and Lakhimpur Battn. A small Party of these under Havildar Sasikarn Rai was attached to the I/4th G.R. and proceeded with them to Gallipoli in August 1915. The remainder of these drafts lefts us in Egypt to join our other Battalion in Mesopotamia.

"It is difficult adequately to express the gallantry, keenness and willing cheerful spirit displayed by the men of the A.M.P. whilst serving with us. They quickly settled down to tranch warfare and conditions utterly unlike any they had formerly experienced, and rapidly identifed themselves with the interests and spirit of the Regt.

"At Neuve Chapelle, Richebourg 9th May and Aubers Ridge 25th September, 1915, they took part in the attacks, showing the utmost gallantry. On the 9th May only two men of the assaulting Brigade reached the German line, both belonged to this Regt and one of them was from the Sadiya Battn. (2nd A.R). It was on this occasion that Jemadar Bakhatman Gurung was killed while leading his platoon in the assault, with Capt. Methew, who had been several years with the Garo and the Naga Hills M.P., was mortally wounded.

"Subadar Mansur Rai (Aijal Battn.) was awarded the Indian Order of Merit for the following act of gallantry:

"On the 25th September, 1915, this Officer led his Company across the parapet in the most gallant manner though exposed to a very heavy fire of rifles and machine guns. Later in the day when the attack was stopped he succeeded in getting his Company back with a number of casualties, and again went out in front of the parapet and was instrumental in bringing in several wounded under the most trying circumstances. Ever since this Officer joined us he has proved himself a capable and gallant leader of men. Awards of the Meritorious Service Medal were subsequently made to the following:

"No. 1443 Havildar Singbir Lama (Lakhimpur Battn).

"No. 1213 Havildar Sasikarn Rai (Lushai Hills Battn).

"The total casualties amongst the men of the A.M.P. while with this Regt were:

"Killed—Jemadar Bakhatman Gurung and 9 other ranks.

"Wounded—18 othter ranks.

"Missing—1 other ranks.

"It is hoped that such survivors may be as proud of their record while serving with us, as this Regt. is proud of its association with such a fine body of men, and for whose willing help and support in such strenuous times this Regt will ever be grateful."

Copy of a letter, No. 4219/V.M.P., of 8.8.21 from the O.C. I/3rd Q.A.O. Goorkha Rifles to the I.G.P. Shillong.

"I beg to give you shortly what my experiences were in connection with the men of the Assam Military Police who joined our 3rd Battn. when it was first raised in Palestine, February 1917, and who served with me. The preliminary organisation was made by Major G.R. Channer, D.S.O., and on my arrival in March I arranged so that all A.M.P. men were kept in their own platoons under their own Officers and N.C.O.'s. All were contented and worked with zeal and keenness, being especially noticeable for their eagerness to learn so that they could the quicker be ready to meet the Hun or the Turk. During the period February to June 1917 some 250 men of the A.M.P. joined us. For the distinctions they won I would refer you to this Regiment's records which at present are with the 2/3rd Goorkha Rifles at Dardoni on the N.W. Frontier.

"I regret I cannot give you further details, but I can assure you that the services rendered by men of the A.M.P. were worthy of their fine traditions and of the parent Regular Battn of the Goorkha Brigade with which they served."

Copy of letter, No. 97/9/110, of 5.8.21, from the O.C. 1/5th Royal Goorkha Rifles to the I.G.P. Shillong.

"Reference your letter No. 44/54 of 27/7/21, I have the honour to reply as follows:

"Not very many men of the Assam Rifles served with this Battn during the war and then only in Mesopotamia, where they never really had a chance of proving their fighting powers. They were however extremely useful in every way, were excellent signallers, and owing to their initiative and resourcefulness were much used by this Battn.

"They identified themselves with us from the beginning, were easy to deal with, and never gave any trouble. Considering the circumstances under which they offered their services and the difficulties (impossible to avoid) which they had to content with, I think their work can only be considered invaluable.

"I tried in 1916 or 1917, in conjunction with Major Molesworth, who had just come from duty with the Assam Military Police, to draw attention to a scheme which I considered useful, by which that Force would be affiliated permanently to the various Goorkha Regts so that in the event of war on a large scale again and the possibility of their services being lent, they might know which units they would be attached to.

"It was hoped that both sides would take more interest in each other during peace, and that in the event of any Assam Riflemen joining their affiliated Battns. they would feel they were going amongst friends. But I never heard more of the matter and did not liik to press it.

"Personally, I consider the Assam Rifles helped the Army greatly in the war, that they would help it again, and I think the desire to effect liaison with them shows perhaps better than anything that their services were really appreciated throughout."

Copy of a letter, No. 1806/D.C./A.T., of 23.8.21, from the O.C. 2/7A Goorkha Rifles to the I.G.P. Shillong.

"Reference your No. 7344-54 of 27.7.21, I would like to address you on the subject of the most excellent work performed by men of the Assam Rifles who were attached to us during the Great War. Drafts from all A.R. units served with us. The first one of 200 rifles joined this Battn. when it was in process of reforming in Mesopotamia after the fall of Kut in April 1916, and you may be pleased to learn that out of nothing we made a Battn again in 5 months, were sent up to join the 3rd Division, and one month later were in action, being the first of the reforming units to go up to the front line again. In December 1916 volunteers were called for to swim the Tigris at night and reconnoitre the Turkish position, 2 men of ours and 2 of the A.R. being chosen. These gallant four set off in the dead of the night in bitterly cold weather, but unfortunately the two Assam Riflemen were drowned in their courageous attempt. I could tell many tales of their bravery and devotion to duty at all times and of their exceptional cheeriness when circumstances were most trying and uncomfortable.

"It was with great regret that I parted with these men on our return to India from Palestine. For four years they had served with my Battn on active service in Mesopotamia and Palestine, and their loyalty, devotion to duty, and gallantry, was beyond praise."

Copy of letter, No. 7/1/219/A of 31/1/22, from the O.C. 1/8th Goorkha Rifles to the I.G.P. Shillong.

"I have asked several of my officers with whom men of the Assam Rifles served during the Great War and who state that the first draft which joined this Battn at Umballa in the pring of 1916 were an exceptionally fine lot and well trained. On service they were at all times willing to like on anything that turned up. The Jaruas amongst them were as willing as any to volunteer for any particular work involving risk. That their services were appreciated by us can be realised from the fact that of all the Indian Orders of Merits granted to us during the War, actual more than half were obtained by men of the Assam or the Burma Military Police.

"To mention idividually, one of the most prominent was Motiram Mech, who gallantly captured a party of Turks single-handed at the battle of Istabulat, 21st April 1917, hunding them out of their trench at the point of his bayonet. the Jaruas were fine athletes and helped us a lot in sport and football, chief amongst them being Subadar Raimat Cachari and Havildar Maniram, both wonderful sprinters and the latter very good at football. In making things cheery during bad times the Jaruas were better than the Goorkhas as singers, dancers, and actors; prominent in this line was one Manmohan Rajbangshi of the 4th A.R.

"To conclude, the old reports of officers on men of the Assam Rifles contain the following terms: smart and soldierly—keen and intelligent—good leader—keen and good Lewis gunner—and so on."

Copy of a letter, No. 27/3/44, of 6.8.21, from the O.C. 1/9th Goorkha Rifles to the I.G.P. Shillong.

"I have the honour to state that a draft from the 1st (Lushai Battn) A.R. joined us in early November 1914, and remained with us till our return from active service in Mesopotamia in 1917. During 1914-!5 in France, although they were in no big actions they were almost continuously in the trenches, and were in 6 small battles. This continued till March 1915, when the 1/9th G.R. took part in the battle of Neuve Chapelle.

"The Battalion was in France till November 1915 and then sailed for Mesopotamia, being twice shelled by submarines during the voyage.

"The 1/9th G.R. returned to India in January 1917, having been continuously on active service for 30 months, and the A.R. draft which was with us throughout lost 7 men killed and 17 wounded. Jemadar Gajman Rai (A.R.) was awarded the I.D.S.M. for gallantry. I have made enquiries from many officers who knew your men well and all agree in saying that they were extremely good material, their standard of training was high, and above all, they were always a credit to this battn during their stay with it."

Copy of letter, No. A.F./2/13 of 29.3.22, from the O.C. I/10th Goorkha Rifles to the I.G.P. Shillong.

"A draft of A.R. volunteers under Subadar Nain Sing Sahi joined this Battn. In Mesopotamia in September 1916 and remained with it until return to India in March 1920.

"The draft of the A.R. did splendid work throughout the whole of the four years they served in Mesopotamia with the unit under my command. Two of the draft obtained the I.D.S.M. for bravery in the field—*viz.* No. 734 Havildar Chandra Singh Chettrie for gallantry in action during the Arab Rebellion of 1920, and No. 1067 Rifleman Karnabahadar Chettrie for gallantry at the battle of Kala Shergat in 1918. The timely arrival of these A.R. volunteers filled a much needed want of trained men in Goorkha Regts. When recruiting was strained to its utmost limits."

Copy of memo., No. 1468/27 of 5.8.21, from the O.C. I/11th Goorkha Rifles to the I.G.P. Shillong.

"Only a few men from the Assam Rifles were transferred to this unit on its formation in Mesopotamia during 1918. All these had previously been serving with the 5th or the 6th Goorkha Rifles. They were re-transferred to Assam very shortly after this unit arrived in India in 1918, so very little was seen of them, but they were excellent men in every way."

Appendix VI

To,

Deputy Commissioner
Khasi and Jaintia Hills

Whereas IU Hain Manick Siem of Mallim, have leased in perpetuity for an annual sum of Rs 20/- the whole tract of land (bounded as under) belonging to the State of Mallim and measuring approximately half a mile by one-fourth mile to the military authorities for the purpose of establishing a regimental colony near Shillong and whereas it is necessary to run over this tract from my jurisdiction as Siem direct control of the Deputy Commissioner of the Khasi and Jaintia Hills in matter relating to civil and criminal jurisdiction. IU Hain Manick Siem, Siem of Malliem give my assent to the said arrangement and understanding fully the term of the agreement do hereby affix my hand and seal the 2nd day of April 1891.

Sd/-

Boundaries

E - by the steep hillock measuring 1520 cubit
W - do measuring 1040 - " -
N - do measuring 1040 - " -
S - by the stream let measuring 169 cubit

Explained to the Siem and understood and agreed by him and given him a copy.

Establishment of Regt. Colony.

DC This is the Patta. I spoke we can take the boundary here given condition & should I think be cancelled.

Bibliography

A. Primary Sources

I. Unpublished

Government Records and Documents:

a. In the National Archives of India, New Delhi.
   Foreign Political Consultations and Proceedings.
   Foreign Secret Consultations and Proceedings.
   Foreign External A Proceedings
   Home Pubic Proceedings
   Home Police Proceedings
   Military Proceedings and Consultations
b. West Bengal State Archives:
   Bengal Judicial Proceedings
   Bengal Political Consultations
c. Assam State Archives, Guwahati
   Letter Issued to Government
   Letters received from Government
   Chief Commissioner's Proceeding—Foreign and Military

II. Published Reports

Bengal Administration Report 1860-1874
Assam Administration Report (Annual)
Assam Police Administration Report (Annual)

Private Papers

Captain G.R. Westmacott: Notes on the History of Assam (Scotland, 1834)
Diary of Sergeant Major George Carter.

B. Secondary Sources

Aitchison, C.U., *Collection of Treaties. Engagements and Sunnads Relating to India and Neighbouring Countries*, Vol. II, (Calcutta, 1863).

Barat, Amiya, *The Bengal Native Infantry. Its Organisation and Discipline 1796-1852*. (Calcutta, 1962).

Banerjee, A.C., *Annexation of Burma*, (Calcutta, 1944).

Banerjee, A.C., *The Eastern Frontier of British India*. (Calcutta, 1964).

Barclay, C.N. (Ed) *The Regimental History of the 3rd Queen Alexandra's Own Gurkha Rifles*, 2 vols, (London, 1953).

Barpujari, H.K., *Problem of the Hill Tribes: North East Frontier*, 3 Vols., (Gauhati, 1969-81).

Barpujari, *Assam in the Days of the Company*, (Gauhati, II Edition, 1983).

Bhatia, H.S., *Military History of British India*, (New Delhi, 1977).

Bhattacharjee, J.B., *Cachar Under British Rule in North East India*, (New Delhi, 1977).

Bista, Dor Bahadur, *The People of Nepal* (Kathmandu, 1967).

Buckland, C.E., *Bengal under the Lieutenant Governors*, Vol. II, (Calcutta, 1901).

Cardew, Lieutenant F.J., *A Sketch of the Services of the Bengal Native Infantry* (Calcutta, 1903).

Carman, W.Y., *Indian Army Uniforms* (London, 1969).

Choudhuri, D.P., *The North East Frontier of India, 1865-1914* (Calcutta, 1979).

Choudhuri, K.C., *Anglo-Nepalese Relations* (Calcutta, 1960), 2 Vols.

Cohen, Stephen, *The Indian Army, Its contribution to the Development of a nation* (London, 1971).

Eden, Ashley, *Political Missions to Bootan* (Reprint, New Delhi, 1972).

Elwin, Verrier, *The Nagas in the Nineteenth Century* (London, 1969).

Farwell, Byron, *Gurkhas* (London, 1984).

Forbes, Duncan, *Johnny Gurkha* (Delhi, 1964).

Fortesque, J.W., *A History of British Army 1815-1838*, Vol. II (London, 1923).

Gait, Edward, *History of Assam* (Calcutta, II Edition, 1927).

Gibbs, H.R.K., *The Gurkha Soldier* (Calcutta, 1943).

Glover, Michael, *An Assemblage of Indian Army Soldier and Uniforms* (London, 1973).

Greaves, Rose Louise, *Persia and the Defence of India, 1884-1892* (London, 1959).

Griffith, Percival, *To Guard My People: History of the Indian Police* (c).

Hasrat, Bikramjit, *History of Nepal* (Chandigarh, 1970).

Hodgson, Brim, *Essays on the Language, Literary and Religion of Nepal and Tibet* (London, 1874), Reprint New Delhi, 1972).

Hussain, Asad, *British India's Relations with the Kingdom of Nepal* (London, 1970).
Hussain, Imdad, "Problem of Defence North-East Frontier (Gauhati University, 1975). (unpblished Ph.D. Thesis).
Hussain, Imdad, "Shan Militia: Origins of the Para-Military System in Assam" in J.B. Bhattacharjee (Ed.) *Studies in the History of North East India* (Shillong, 1986).
Huxford, H.L., *History of the 8th Gurkha Rifles, 1824-47*, (Aldershot, 1952).
Karan, P.P. and Jenkins, W.M., *The Himalayan Kingdom* (Princeton, 1963).
Lamb, Alistair, *Britain and Chinese Central Asia* (London, 1960).
Landon, P., *Nepal*, 2 Vols. (London, 1928).
Longer, V., *Red Costs to Olive Green, A History of the Indian Army, 1600-1974* (New Delhi, 1974).
Mackenzie, Alexander, *The North East Frontier of India*, (1984, Reprint 1979, 1980, 1981).
Macenzie, A., *A History of the Relation of the Government with the Hill Tribes on the North East Frontier of Bengal,* (Calcutta, 1884).
Macmunn, George, *The Martial Races of India* (London, reprinted New Delhi, 1972).
Majumdar, Lieutenant Colonel B.N., *History of the Army Service Corps 1858 1913* (New Delhi, 1976).
Mason, Philip, *A Matter of Honour, An Account of the Indian Army, Its Officers and Men* (Norwich, 1974).
Mehra, P.L., *McMohan Line and After* (Madras, 1974).
Messerschmidt, D.A., *The Gurungs of Nepal* (New Delhi, 1976).
Michell, St. John F. Captain, *Report on the North East Frontier of India* (Calcutta, 1883).
Mills, A.J. Moffat, *Report on Assam* (Calcutta, 1854).
Mishra, B.B., *Administrative History of India*, (London, 1970).
Mojumdar, Kanchanmoy, *Political Relations between India and Nepal, 1877-1923* (New Delhi, 1973).
Mojumdar, K., *Anglo-Nepalese Relations in the 19th century* (Calcutta, 1973).
Morris, C.J., *The Gurkhas: A Handbook for the Indian Army* (Delhi, 1933).
Muktan, K.K., *The Legendary Gorkhas*, 2002, Guwahati.
Northey, W.B. and Morris, C.J. *The Gurkhas, Their Manners, Customs and Country* (London, 1928, Indian Reprint 1974).
Oldfield, HA, *Sketches from Nepal*, 2 Vols. (London, 1880, Reprint New Delhi, 1974).
Pal, Dharam, *Tradition of the Indian Army* (Delhi, 1961).
Palit, D.K., *Sentinels of the North East* (The Assam Rifles) (New Delhi, 1984).
Palsokar, R.O. *History of the 5th Gorkha Rifles* (*Frontier Force*). (Shillong 1991).

Pemble, *John The Invasion of Nepal, John Company at war* (Oxford University Press 1971).

Pemberton *Report on the Eastern Frontier of British India.*

Pradhan, K.L. *"Brian Hodgson at the Kathmandu Residency"* (North Eastern Hill University, 1986). (unpublished Ph.D. Thesis).

Rahul, Ram. *The Himalayan Borderland* (New Delhi, 1970).

Ramakant. *Indo-Nepalese Relations,* (New Delhi, 1968).

Regmi, D.R. *Ancient Nepal* (Calcutta, 1960).

Regi, D.R. *Modern Nepal* (Calcutta, 1960).

Reid, Sir Robert *History of the Frontier Areas Borderina on Assam 1883-1941* (Delhi, 1942).

Reid, Surgeon Lieutenant Colonel A.S. *Chin Lushai Land* (Calcutta, 1983).

Rennie, D.F. *shotan and the story of the Doar War* (London, 1866).

Robert, Lord, *Forty One Years In India* (London, 1897).

Rose, Leo, *Nepal Strategy for Survival* (Berkeley, 1971).

Rose, L.E. and Fisher, M.W., *The Politics of Nepal* (Ithaca, New York, 1970).

Rustomji, N.K. and Ramble, C. (Ed.) *Himalayan Environment and Culture* (New Delhi, 1990).

Ryan, D.G.J., *Historical Records of the 6th Gorkha Rifles, 1817-1919* (Aldershot, 1925).

Sanwal, B.D., *Nepal-East India Company* (Bombay, 1965).

Saxena, K.M.L., *The Military System of India, 1850-1900* (New Delhi, 1974).

Shakespear, Colonel L.W., *History of the Assam Rifles* (London, 1929).

Shakespear, Colonel L.W., *History of the 2nd King Edward's Own Goorkha Rifles* (The Sirmoor Rifles), (Aldershot, 1912/24).

Singh, Hiralal, *Problems and Policies of British in India* (1963).

Sinha, A.C., Subba, T.B., *Nepalies in the North East India*, (Delhi, 2003).

Spate, O.H.K., Learmouth, A.T.A. and Farmer, B.H. *India, Pakistan and Ceylon: The Regions*, (New Delhi, 1972).

Stiller, Ludwig F., *The Rise of the House of Gorkha* (Patna, 1973).

Syiemlieh, D.R., *British Administration in Meghalaya* (New Delhi, 1989).

Tucker, Francis, *The Gurkha Brigade and the Story of Gurkhas in Nepal* (London, 1957).

Vansittart, Eden, *Gurkhas* (Calcutta, 1915).

Wilson, H.H., *Documents Illustrative of the Burmese War* (Calcutta, 1827).

Woodthorpe, R.G., *The Lushai Expedition, 1871-1872* (London, 1873).

Woodyatt, Nigel, *Regimental History of the 3rd Queen Alexandra's Own Gurkha Rifles* (London, 1929).

Index